Drinking to Kindness

A Decade of Madness on the Big Sur Coast

by Kristin Cameron

PublishAmerica
Baltimore

© 2005 by Kristin Cameron.
All rights reserved. No part of this book may be reproduced, stored in a retrieval system, or transmitted in any form or by any means without the prior written permission of the publishers, except by a reviewer who may quote brief passages in a review to be printed in a newspaper, magazine, or journal.

First printing

Cover: *View from Partington*, a watercolor by Robin Coventry.

Author photo by Judy McPhail.

Permission to quote John Robinson Jeffers has been granted by Jeffers Literary Properties.

The Barbara Spring article first appeared in *Big Sur Women*, edited by Judith Goodman, copyright 1985.

ISBN: 1-4137-6297-2
PUBLISHED BY PUBLISHAMERICA, LLLP
www.publishamerica.com
Baltimore

Printed in the United States of America

To Alice

Dedication

*For my children, who weathered the madness.
For Mutti, who kept buying me typewriter
ribbons and paper and urging me to write.
For my husband, Alan, who gave me the love
and support to do it.
And for Keeker, because without her, none
of this would have happened.*

*from your long time fan,
Kristin*

In Memory of:

Robin Coventry
Harrydick Ross
Bill Spring
Paige Binker
Richard Trotter
Frank, Fern, and Walter Trotter

Table of Contents

I Big Sur	...9
II Commode-Hugging Drunk	...15
III Harrydick Ross	...23
IV Confronting the Earth Spirit	...28
V Paradise Lost	...37
VI Trouble Shooting	...46
VII Will the Real Miss Woods Please Stand Up	...53
VIII Keeking	...58
IX Binker	...65
X Easy Street	...70
XI Future King of Scots	...75
XII Poets and Painters	...80
XIII Chewey	...85
XIV Laurel and Hardy Construction	...89
XIV Out of the Frying Pan, Into the Fire	...92
XVI Santa Lucia Ranch	...99
XVII Bed and Breakfast	...104
XVIII E.I.E.I.O.	...109
XIX Prisoners of Freedom	...113
XX Oh, Holy Night	...116
XXI Motherlode	...121
XXII Church in the Wildwood	...125
XXIII Rocky Creek Barn	...130
XXIV To Climb and Fall	...134

1
Big Sur

"Black Betty had a baby, bam-be-lam
The damn thing gone crazy, bam-be-lam
It was born in a mine, bam-be-lam
The damn thing gone blind, bam-be-lam
Woe, Woe, Woe, Black Betty, bam-be-lam
I said, Woe Black Betty, bam-be-lam"

It was the summer of 1967 and the six of us were off for a wild weekend in the old green Ford van. In the back, on a pile of sleeping bags and backpacks were Barry Milo, Psycho Rick, and Big Babs. In the front seat driving the van was my boyfriend, Carlton, with me next to him and Weird Ward by the window.

He was the one playing the harmonica and stamping the floorboards singing "Black Betty." Big Sur had been his idea. None of the rest of us had ever been there before but we were up for any kind of an adventure that happened along. Trouble was, we'd gotten the idea to go camping at around nine o'clock in the evening when we were all a little high, and none of us, not even Ward, who claimed he'd been there a couple of times before, could remember how far away from San Francisco Big Sur was.

The drive seemed endless. Two, three, four hours went by, and Ward kept playing the same song over and over again, beating his big old motorcycle boots on the floor. Milo was snoring, Rick was half-ass strumming his guitar and Babs was getting antsy. Finally she announced that she'd held out for as long as she could and if we didn't stop and let her pee it was gonna be bam-be-lam all over the sleeping bags.

We were winding along the cliff tops of Highway One now, somewhere on the Big Sur coast. Ward said he knew a campground. He didn't remember the name of it but he'd know it when he saw it. Since it was about one o'clock in the morning and so foggy we could barely see two feet ahead, we had our doubts.

Carlton finally saw something that looked as if it might be a pullout and eased the old Ford off the road. Babs wasted no time in jumping out the side door.

Carlton rolled down his window and let some of the fog blow in. "Pass that wine jug up, will you, Ricky," he called into the back. We all had a gulp or two of Red Mountain Burgundy. Milo had bought the jug since he was the only one of us over twenty-one.

"Any cigarettes left back there?" Ward asked. The cigarettes were passed forward. The night was still except for the sound of waves crashing against giant rocks somewhere far below us.

"Henry Miller lives around here someplace, doesn't he?" Ward said, peering out into the fog.

"Is he the guy who married Marilyn Monroe?" Rick asked.

"No, that was Arthur," I said. "Henry's the one that writes dirty books."

"Hmmm," said Rick. "I'd like to look him up." Rick saw a psychiatrist once a week and it was rumored that he had sex with his sister.

Ward played a few more stanzas of "Black Betty" and we passed the jug around again.

"What the hell's keeping her, I wonder?" said Carlton.

Ward rolled down the window. "Hey Babsy! You constipated or

what? We wanta get going."

We listened, but all we could hear was the wind blowing the fog through the redwood trees, and the sound of surf crashing on distant rocks.

And then there was something else, like the low moan of a sleepy elephant seal on some invisible beach far below.

We all got out of the car. All but Milo who was still asleep. "Hey, Babs, are you out there?" we shouted. And the sound came again…drifting up on the mist.

For an instant the wind blew the fog aside long enough for us to see that we were parked right on the edge of a cliff. In her haste, Babs had leapt out of the van and presumably over the edge of what appeared to be about a 600-foot drop.

"Shit," said Carlton. "I wonder if I have any rope. Somebody wake up Barry. He was in the Navy."

"What the hell good is that going to do?" Rick asked.

"Well, he knows life saving and how to tie knots and stuff."

But Barry was pretty drunk and he only groaned and muttered when we pounded on him, so in the end we pulled Babs up the cliff with a series of bungy cords and blankets tied together.

It turned out that she was cut and bruised and terrified, but nothing was broken as she had gotten caught on a cascara bush halfway down. We tried to cheer her up by reminding her that she HAD come for an adventure, and we let her drink the rest of the wine so she'd calm down a bit.

At long last we located Lime Kiln Campground which had a sign on the gatepost saying it was closed. That we ignored. The gate was open and there didn't seem to be any park attendants or rangers around at that hour of the morning, so we drove down to the beach and rolled out our sleeping bags in the sand.

It seemed like only a few hours later that we woke up to find ourselves and our belongings soaking wet and being carried out to sea. It was dawn and the tide had come in.

Cursing and shivering we retrieved our floating pillow and jackets and moved up to higher ground. As the day grew lighter and people began to move around, we saw that the campground was not state or nationally owned, but seemed to be operated and patronized by grizzly looking mountain men and homeless hippies living in VW vans and old school buses.

Milo was sent off down the road to a store for more wine and some salami and cheese and we spent the day quite happily drying off, playing music and jamming with some of the other campers.

Later on, for reasons we never did learn, the outhouse, which was located not far from our campsite, exploded. Hot shit flew like molten lava all over us and the other unlucky campers who had parked themselves near the restroom for convenience sake.

We headed back to the city Sunday morning, sunburned, hung over, and reeking from the thousands of airborne particles that the exploding outhouse had embedded in our gear. We had had enough adventure for one weekend.

The next time I went to Big Sur was seven years later. I was eight months pregnant, and I was with my husband and our friend, Keeker, who had just purchased a house from her Aunt Maud. The house was located high on a hill called Partington Ridge, and none of us had ever been there before.

Keeker had been a neighbor of mine during my teenage years. She was a wealthy heiress to a railroad fortune, but she had chosen to live in a small house in the woods next door to the house my mother and I lived in. She was a bra and draft card burner, ready to argue any issue and question all authority. She owned her own bar, advocated the legalization of drugs, and knew all sorts of exotic people.

When I was fifteen she had been a wild woman and my mentor, but now, eleven years later she had suffered an aneurysm which had left her right side totally paralyzed. She felt that the remote peace and quiet of a Big Sur retreat would be just what she needed while she regained her strength.

Keeker was in the back seat reading out her Aunt Maud's

DRINKING TO KINDNESS

directions to the house, and my husband, Robin, a Scottish artist who I had met and married while going to drama school in Scotland, was sitting in the passenger seat beside me complaining about the fact that the fog was starting to blow in and he had wanted to do a watercolor while we were here. He didn't drive because he claimed American highways "went for his stomach." Lots of things had this effect on him, including pork chops, large crowds and the sight of his own blood.

Seeing the steep sea cliffs and the fog blowing in took me back to that fateful night in 1967. "I hear Henry Miller lives around here someplace," I said.

"Is he the one that was married to Marilyn Monroe?" Robin asked.

"No, he's the one that's always writing about cunts," snapped Keeker. "Cunts, cunts, cunts. Diddle, diddle, diddle. I believe his house is supposed to be right next to mine. Pull over here. I think that's the road."

"Jesus Christ!" I said, looking at a goat trail that wound steeply up the side of a mountain. "Surely not."

We checked the map again and that was indeed the Partington Ridge road. The directions said it was paved, but if there was any sort of a surface on it, it must have been done back in 1937 when they built the coastal highway. The baby somersaulted and quivered uneasily in my stomach, and Robin groaned.

"Well, I hope we don't meet anyone coming down," I said. "Here goes."

I began winding my way cautiously up the narrow road when I suddenly caught sight in the rear view mirror of a BMW racing up the hill toward us at great speed. The driver, who appeared to be a woman, began to honk and shake her fist at us as she got closer. I tried to remain calm, skidding along the steep gravel, and as soon as I came to something that vaguely resembled a pullout, hanging over a 1,000 foot drop, I edged over. This allowed the woman to squeeze up next to us, where she rolled down her window and began to scream with uncontrolled anger.

"Can't you assholes read?" she yelled. "Didn't you see the

goddamn sign? This is a private fucking road!"

I cleared my throat and smiled sweetly while the others stared in amazement. "This is Ms. Dorcy," I said. "She has just purchased the Maud Oakes' house here on the ridge. I believe it's located somewhere near Henry Miller's home."

The woman thought this information over in silence for a minute. Finally she said, "Well then, I guess that makes us neighbors. I'm Valentine Miller, Henry's daughter."

"How charming," said Keeker. "And fuck you, too."

The BMW zoomed past us and on up the mountain.

"Keeker needs a joint now," she said, fumbling in the picnic basket packed full of goodies which we had hoped to enjoy out on the new patio overlooking the sea. "I can't cope. I'm not ready for this place. Someday I'll be stronger, but not now. I can't possibly deal with this road and that aggressive woman. I'd be so intimidated that I'd have to be stoned all the time and then I'd fall off the mountain and end up in the hospital again. No, no. You two can come and live in the house and take care of it for the summer. Robby can paint lots of nice pictures. I'll come down again at Christmas time when I'm feeling stronger."

And so it was that the third time I came to Big Sur, it was with Robin and our six-week-old son, Jamie, with good old Mad Milo at the wheel of a U-Haul truck. It was a summer holiday that was to go on for the next ten years.

99
Commode-Hugging Drunk

I first met my friend Barry Milo in Men's Underwear at the Stanford Emporium in Palo Alto, California. He was freshly out of the Navy and had only been in Men's Underwear for a day or two when we ran across one another over a display of argyle socks.

He was very short, with thin dark hair and horn-rimmed glasses, and was such a contrast to all of the long-haired, bearded, folk-rock freaks that I was accustomed to being around, that for ten minutes or so we didn't know we had anything in common besides argyle socks. I think I finally said that I had been to Argyle in Scotland, where the socks originated, and he asked me if everyone ate fish and chips over there. I said yes, and that I was currently singing at a folk music place that served fish and chips in downtown Palo Alto. He got all excited and said he played a banjo and we were off and running. Within a week he had abandoned Men's Underwear and gotten a job as fry cook at the folk club, and we've been friends ever since.

It seemed like in those days whenever we'd get together all kinds of insane things would happen, possibly due to the fact that we drank quite a lot. One night we crashed into, and wrapped the VW bug around, a railroad-crossing sign. Even though the front and back sides of the car were both facing the same direction we somehow managed to drive it home.

The next car he got we accidentally drove off of Rattlesnake Mountain one night when we were out chopping down housing development signs in the hills behind Stanford University. After we'd climbed out of the car and back up the hill again, Barry insisted on being lowered back down by rope to retrieve his ten-gallon Stetson hat from the back seat. He claimed that without it he felt much too short.

With this kind of history, I should have known better than to ask Barry to drive the U-Haul van when we moved to Big Sur, but I was in a bind with Robin not being able to drive and me with the new baby. Anyway, he was the only one who volunteered to help.

A year before, Robin and I had arrived from Scotland with two suitcases and now, thanks to well-meaning relatives who had come to our rescue like a giant swap meet, we had become overwhelmed with things they no longer needed. We now owned old chairs, a picnic table, faded bedspreads, chipped dishes, a vacuum cleaner that wouldn't cost much to fix, but no carpet to use it on, and a crib for the baby that collapsed on an average of three times a night.

In addition to all this, Keeker had decided to use her new house as a storage place for things she wasn't using in her home in the woods, one of which was a huge walnut desk weighing about three hundred pounds, on which, she assured me, she would some day write the great American novel.

I called a U-Haul dealer and tried to explain about the steep, twisty one-lane road, low-hanging branches, falling rocks, and all. The girl in the office said that she would do her best. I had in mind something bigger than a Volkswagen bus, but smaller than a Winnebago motor home.

Old Mad Milo came over the night before the move and we packed boxes, sipping and singing; toasting our good fortune, our friendship, and our future.

The next morning we arrived bright and early at the U-Haul place, which turned out to be a small, sleazy-looking gas station, and there was only one truck in the lot behind it. The truck appeared to be about twenty-four feet long and maybe twelve feet high, like a full-fledged moving van.

Robin immediately announced that he was going by bus and would meet us in Monterey tomorrow.

"You'll do no such thing," I said.

The baby, sensing that something was wrong, began to cry, and Barry walked round and round the truck, giggling and kicking the tires, muttering, "Jesus H. Christ."

I went into the office and tried to explain that there had been some mistake, but the only person there was a greasy little mechanic who claimed he "didn't know nothin' about it."

"Da boss lef me da keys an da papers and sez you gotta have her back by Sunday night," he said.

"But we'll never make it in that thing!" I wailed. "It's far too big. I asked for something small, like a UPS van or something. It's a steep, one-lane road with blind corners."

The mechanic shrugged. "Dat's da only truck we got, lady," he said. "Take it or leave it."

Reluctantly, I filled out the papers, wrote the man a check and took the keys. I had no ideas how we were going to get there, but we were all packed and ready to move, so I figured we might just as well go for it, ludicrous as it might be.

Barry was attempting to get into the driver's seat, but having failed to be able to reach the first step up, he was now making little running jumps at it. "Does this thing come with a step ladder?" he asked the man.

"It's got a radio," the man replied.

"Does it have a dashboard Jesus?" I asked. "I have a feeling we'll be wanting to do a lot of praying." I felt like a third-world astronaut, blasting off in a ship that would almost certainly never make it to the moon.

Our first stop, before we even packed the truck, was the liquor store. We bought some beer and wine, and as an afterthought, Barry added a bottle of brandy for courage.

When we began to load up the truck, it became obvious that what had looked like a lot of possessions the night before was only going to take up about a third of this huge vehicle. Barry suggested that we could probably fit our apartment in the truck, too, if we'd like to take it along.

The trip took four hours. Robin, on the passenger side, jumped and squealed for the first hour and refused to open his eyes for the next three. I sat in the middle trying to comfort the baby. Barry at the helm kept the country and western station going full blast to drown out reality. Every now and then he'd take his hand off the wheel to play along on an invisible air guitar. The truck would swerve. I would scream, Robin would moan, and we'd pop another beer.

It was late afternoon by the time we arrived at the foot of Partington Ridge and we were all half drunk, tired and grumpy.

"Well, there's the road, you maniac!" I snapped at Barry. "Get ready to meet your maker."

Barry just sat there and stared for a minute, and then he switched off the ignition and the country and western music. The baby had fallen asleep and we all three sat there in silence, listening to the waves break 400 feet below us.

"Shiiiiiiit," Barry whispered. "Ain't no fuckin' way this thing's gonna make it up there."

"Well, it just simply has to," I stated matter-of-factly. "That's all there is to it. If not, I'm going to arrange the furniture in the back of this truck and live at this pullout for the rest of my life."

"I'm going to walk up," Robin whimpered. "Please, luv, let's just have a wee rest and think about this. Maybe there will be someone with a smaller truck and we can shuttle it up the hill, eh?"

"Oh, for Christ's sake, stop whimpering," I said. "We aren't going to shuttle, and you aren't going to walk. If we die, we all die together. Now open the window and stick your head out to make sure the tires are staying on the road as we go up."

"Bloody Americans!" Robin hissed. "A lot of bloody fools. My stomach cannae take this."

"OK," said Barry, squaring his shoulders. "Let's share that brandy."

I rummaged around in the grocery bag full of empty beer cans and passed him the bottle. He took a long pull at it, and then started up the engine. "Let the good times roll," he said.

There wasn't even as much as a quarter of an inch of road to spare on either side, and half the time only one of the dual tires was on the ground and the other was hanging out in space. Slowly, slowly, we inched our way up, knocking out sage brush and greasewood, crushing culvert pipes and guard rails in an effort to stay on track. I prayed that Valentine Miller would not come roaring down around a turn in her little BMW.

A mile and a quarter up, the road made a left turn into a safer looking section lined with oak trees and we paused for a sigh of relief. The brandy was passed around one more time and we all congratulated Barry on a job well done. Sweat was pouring out from under his cowboy hat, and he had to take off his glasses and mop his face.

"Not much further now," I assured him. "Half a mile at the most."

"I don't know how the hell we made it," Barry said. "It's just a damn good thing we didn't meet anybody coming down."

Feeling a bit more confident now that our journey was almost over, we started off again, a little faster this time. It was not long after that the crash came. A wood-splintering, metal-tearing, wrenching sort of sound came from overhead. The truck jolted to a halt and we all looked at each other. The baby woke up and began to cry.

Robin was first out, only too glad to desert us all. From the look on his face, Barry was reluctant to get out and check the damage, but after one more swig, he climbed down, jumping the three feet to the ground.

"Son of a bitch," he said, eying the top of the truck. "Is this thing insured?"

I shuffled through my purse looking for the papers that the mechanic had given me. I finally found them and started skimming through all the red tape. "Let's see…collision…blah, blah, blah…it looks like it's covered for everything except overhead damage," I said.

"That's not good news," said Barry. "You better have a look at this."

It seemed that in an effort to keep our eyes peeled to the side of the road, we had neglected to look up and remember the height of the truck. He had driven directly into a huge, low-hanging limb of an oak tree. It had penetrated the highest section of the wood and aluminum frame, known as "Mom's Attic" and come to rest inside the van on one of Keeker's brown corduroy sofa beds like an uninvited guest.

This was not the entrance I had meant to make into our peaceful new surroundings, but like it or not we were about to meet all the new neighbors. The crash had echoed down the canyon and now curious people started to appear from seemingly invisible driveways and houses. One lady asked if she could hold the baby, and a man ran back home to get a chain saw. Everyone laughed and shook their heads at the great folly of trying to bring such an impossible vehicle up the ridge road.

Half an hour more and the truck was freed and ready to drive the last quarter of a mile up the trail to our new home.

We were to have the caretaker's quarters on the property, a one-room, studio-type house with a loft bedroom and bath. Unfortunately it could only be reached by climbing up a steep flight of concrete steps from the main house, and in our present state of exhaustion, we decided to bring in only a few of the essentials and leave the major unloading for later. Groceries, diapers, dishes and the crib were hauled up the stairs, and then the celebration began.

I'm not sure how long it went on. Bottles blended into hours and hours into days. We watched the sunset and wept and a blanket caught fire and someone threw up on the geraniums. Robin kept talking about whales, and I was scanning the horizon saying, "Whales…whales…white whales in the sunset." But I couldn't see any.

Someone changed the baby and put him to bed, and someone cooked pork chops, and someone threw the wine glasses in the fireplace. And at some point I woke up outside, in the dark, all cold and wet, and wondered where the hell I was. Way off to my left I could hear someone singing and the sound was echoing out over the canyon like a coyote howling at the moon.

"Rooock me maaaamaaa. Rooock me aaaaall night loonggg. Wantcha ta rooock me maaamaaa, like ma back ain't got no booone."

I got up and did a sort of samba over to where the voice was coming from and found old Mad Milo lying in a compost heap cuddled up to a moldy head of cabbage.

"Let's get together for a little poozle," he whispered to it. "You and me and a little walk on the wild side."

This was a pretty pathetic sight and I decided I had better sober up and take charge before he got too intimate with the compost.

"Hey, buddy boy," I said, shivering in the dampness. "What say we go in and have a wee cup of tea and get ourselves pulled together."

"Jesus Christ," said Barry, rolling over on his back. "I'm as horny as a hoot owl."

Inside the house we found Robin asleep in the bathroom with one arm draped fondly around the toilet bowl.

"Now that's what I call commode-hugging drunk," said Barry. "Downright disgusting."

We drank tea, made toast, heated up a can of baked beans and sat watching the dawn come up over the Santa Lucia Mountains. By some miracle the baby was still warm and happy in his crib that had managed for once not to collapse.

"I wonder what day it is?" I said.

"Several days later than it used to be," said Barry. "Shit, I have to get to work."

"I have to get this truck back. God, what the hell am I going to tell them? We don't have any money to pay for all that damage. We're screwed."

"Maybe I'll drive it off a cliff somewhere out by Davenport and hitch a ride home," Barry said.

"Yeah, I'll just tell them the truck got stolen," I said, getting excited. "That's a great idea."

"Anyway, I better get going before there's too much traffic on the road," Barry said, gathering up his things. "Tell the old Scotsman I said, 'Cheerio.'"

"Hey, Barry, wait a minute. There's something we should do before you dump that truck," I said.

"Yeah, what's that?"

"Unload it."

III
Harrydick Ross

We hadn't been on the ridge more than a week when Harrydick Ross called and invited us over for drinks. The telephone had just been connected half an hour earlier and I had not even looked at the number, much less tried to memorize it, and already it was ringing. A wonderful deep voice at the other end of the line said, "Hello, honey. The Rosses would like to invite you for cocktails at five."

"Would it be all right if I brought the baby?" I asked.

"We ADORE babies," he said.

"Wonderful. We'll be there. And thank you!"

Harrydick Ross, who claimed to have been born on the back of a mule on the Old Chisholm Trail, was somewhat of a legend in Big Sur. How he had come to have the name Harrydick, and why anyone with that name would chose to use it was something that I always wondered, but never had the nerve to ask. Perhaps, as my father suggested, it paid to advertise.

Harrydick and his wife, Lillian Boss Ross, whom he always referred to as "Shanagolden," an Irish nickname he had given her, had come to Big Sur from San Francisco in the thirties before the highway was built. He had been a young sculptor, and she, a writer. They had hiked and camped and lived in many of the old cabins and homesteads, including the cottage at Livermore Ledge where Lillian wrote *The Stranger*, which was later made into a movie with Liv Ulman, called *Zande's Bride*. Finally they settled on Partington Ridge, building their little home out of brick and block and whatever bits and pieces happened along. It faced southwest toward the rolling ridges of the Santa Lucias and the sunset, and Henry Miller's house was the next one down the road.

After Lillian died, Henry's second wife, Eve, divorced him and moved next door to marry Harrydick. Eve, who was an ex-Hollywood actress, had a delicate touch with figure drawing and etching. She worked closely with another local artist friend of theirs, a widow named Helen Colby. For awhile the three of them had a productive artists' workshop going on in the backyard studio until Eve tragically died one night from an overdose of bourbon and valium.

Harrydick then married Helen, who he always referred to as "Colby," but his heavy drinking and smoking habits soon sent her off to live in her own house about thirty miles north in the Carmel Highlands. Harrydick went to visit her on weekends, and claimed that when he was there they drank only green tea.

By the time we met him, he was living alone, but he always referred to himself as "we." At seventy-nine, he claimed to be able to out-drink, out-smoke, out-sing and out-seduce any of the "young uns." We were greeted at the door with open arms and good strong martinis, and to Jamie, who was peeking at him out of the backpack, he sang a few stanzas of, "Babes in the woods, poor babes in the woods."

Everywhere there were wonderful things to see. On one wall was a huge fresco of two nudes done by Eve and Helen. Another wall was all bookshelves, floor to ceiling, with books of all kinds, from shabby paperbacks to old leather bound volumes. There were carved torsos, mobiles, colored glass and chiseled rock and wood.

Outside the window, a collection of copper pipe bells were chiming. Beyond them the hollyhocks and morning glories grew up around carved bridge timbers, manzanita burls and metal sculptures of women and serpents.

DRINKING TO KINDNESS

Harrydick raised his glass. "Around here we only drink to one thing," he said. "Kindness."

We drank to kindness, and we drank to the Scots, and then we went out to the studio...past the little pond and the overgrown steps, the potting shed, the tangerine tree, and the ironwood carved head of John the Baptist.

The studio was as wonderful as the house. A life-sized Egyptian Cleopatra-like figure hung from the ceiling. A mobile of old spectacle lenses sent prism colors dancing on walls lined with pastel paintings of geese, sketches of nudes and sailing ships made from old window shutters.

In the workshop were hundreds of antique tools, a wood stove made of old tire rims and a sculpture in progress of a one-breasted woman.

"One of her breasts cracked, so I had to give her a mastectomy," Harrydick said sadly. "But she's just as gorgeous with one as she was with two, don't you think?"

And then Robin spotted Eve's etching press. It had been his dream, his constant complaint, his daily promise, "If only I had an etching press...when I get an etching press...I can't express the right mood without an etching press...." And now here was an art studio, a lonely artist and an etching press, all within walking distance of our new home.

"We could get a workshop together...an art club...etching, drawing, carving...poetry and music...like Paris in the twenties," Robin began to babble, and Harrydick's old eyes started to sparkle. "We'd better have another martini," he said.

It didn't take long for the workshop to get underway. For some reason it consisted exclusively of females buzzing with energy and bursting with creative inspiration, while Robin proudly stood at the wheel of the press, like a ship's captain, shouting orders to his crew of eager etchers.

I wasn't much interested in learning to etch. I would go sit in Harrydick's house, at the big desk, nursing the baby and checking out the old leather bound books. In front of me on the table was a datebook open to July 24, 1958. It said, "Dine at Roosevelts', 5:00 p.m."

"What was I doing on July 24 in 1958?" I wondered. I was 11 years old, living in Germany with my cousins. And all the time I was growing up, Harrydick was here, watching the canyons change color in the evening and dining with his neighbor, Nicholas Roosevelt, a cousin of Teddy, as he was still doing every Thursday night. Maybe that's why he never bothered getting a new date book.

I wandered out to the workshop to see how the artists were getting on. Harrydick was giving a lecture on the word "FUCK," which some disappointed prodigy must have just uttered. "It's a perfectly good AngloSaxon term," he was saying. "There is nothing wrong with the word, 'Fuck.' Now 'SHIT' is a swear word, and you must never, never use that term. Of course, I just prefer to say 'BALLS,' myself."

"Look!" Robin cried happily. "The bubbles are starting to appear on the zinc plates." He put his hand over his heart as if to offer a pledge of allegiance, or perhaps to quiet it from racing out of control. "This is always the most exciting moment to me...when those bubbles start to appear."

Harrydick turned to me and shook his head sadly. "If that's what excites him, honey," he said, "you'd better come and live with me."

After the workshop, Harrydick invited everyone in for drinks. Marilyn Abel had brought over a bottle of Drambuie, which had already been utilized in the studio. A successful print was rewarded with a shot glass full of liqueur, and losers got double. The less talented members of the group, who had taken a lot of unsuccessful prints, were already high flying.

We fired up the old record player and Marilyn did a little elfin dance. Karin Wynar tried to demonstrate that by pushing hard on Harrydick's head we could make him levitate, only he never did. Robin did the highland fling, and I invited everyone to stay for spaghetti, only somehow there were none of the right ingredients around.

At three o'clock in the morning, I woke up with my head on

Harrydick's knee. He was snoring away in his chair, with a drink still in his hand, and Robin was calypsoing around in a corner, holding the sleeping baby. On the record player Harry Belafonte had gotten stuck in a rut, God knows how long ago, and he was crying, "Day-o, Day-o, Day-o, Day-o," over and over again. I dragged myself to my feet. "Daylight come and me wanta go home," I said, finishing his sentence for him.

Later that morning I had one of the worst hangovers I could ever remember, but guilt compelled me to gather my wits together and hike down the hill to help Harrydick clean up the mess we'd left. I hoped that perhaps he might still be asleep and I could just creep in, like the tooth fairy, do the dishes, tidy up and leave a thank you note under his pillow, but when I got there he was standing in the kitchen wearing nothing but a T-shirt, and drinking a cup of coffee.

"Was it a good party, honey?" he asked me.

"It was a fine party!" I said.

"The only thing left in the liquor cupboard is a bottle of Dubonet," he said. "I'll go put on some pants and you can pour us each a drink. We'll open a can of caviar. It'll be a hell of a breakfast!"

I very nearly gagged. Dubonnet and caviar! My stomach hadn't even felt strong enough yet for a cup of tea, but I gritted my teeth and did as I was told, carrying a tray out to the porch, where the sun was just beginning to filter through the pine trees.

Harrydick came out behind me, chuckling to himself. "You know, honey, over the years I've waked up to find a lot of different things beside my bed the morning after. Ladies' stockings and panties, high heels and slips, but this morning I woke up and there was a pair of baby booties and a diaper on the pillow next to me. I said to myself, "Oh Christ, Ross, what have you done now!"

IV
Confronting the Earth Spirit

There is a path that climbs up and around the back of our house, through the pine trees and up to a clearing where you can see the ridges, one after another, reaching down to the sea, like a herd of sleeping dinosaurs, all the way to Nepenthe and on rare occasions to Point Sur. It was on this path that I would get funny feelings, excitement, terror, goose bumps, tingling, like I was being watched. Not just watched, but scrutinized sarcastically, like a pimply freshman girl being checked out by the senior football team.

I would whirl around and try to catch someone peeking at me from behind a tree, but they were too clever. I knew they were there because I caught them a few times, jumping back just as I'd turn around. Smug tricksters that whispered just low enough that I could not make out what they were saying.

The path was slippery because of the thick layer of pine needles that covered it and so I usually navigated it barefoot, using my feet as primal claws, curling and scooping my toes into the ground to keep from falling. It was due to being barefoot that I discovered the one place on the path that was always warm, even when the sun had not shone all day.

I began to stop there and sit awhile whenever I climbed the path.

DRINKING TO KINDNESS

I remembered reading about ley lines when I lived in Scotland. Places like energy bands on or inside the earth where sacred wells and shrines had stood since time immemorial; where animals went year after year to give birth to their young; where brave young knights had disappeared into fairy mounds, and reappeared fifty years later looking not a day older than when they vanished. Spiritual spots, time warps, places of magnitude like Stonehenge and the pyramids...infinite giants that had been there forever, but nobody could figure out why.

I had heard that Big Sur was a high energy spot on the planet like Tibet and Macchu Pichu, so perhaps I had discovered a ley line. It was sitting on this spot that I saw my first whale; a huge California gray, cresting and spouting off the shore 1,000 feet below. It absolutely took my breath away and I wanted to call out to it, but I simply couldn't speak. Behind me the whisperers were conversing. They had sensed my excitement. Once more I turned quickly, thinking that maybe this time they might show themselves, but they were gone again and silent.

I wondered if this happened all over Big Sur, and if everyone just accepted it. Were the whispers from ghostly spirits, or was it the trees themselves, or perhaps the devas of the multicolored wildflowers that grew all over the hillside. Pale pink buckwheat, orange sticky monkey weed and bright red Indian paint brush. I decided to listen a little more closely and to check out the other local residents for signs of enlightenment.

Since moving in, I had rarely ever seen Valentine Miller and it turned out that Henry had long since moved south to Pacific Palisades, but there was a young man living at the Miller's acting as a sort of caretaker. He was around twenty, tall, fair, wide-eyed and expressionless, like someone under a hypnotic spell. Every night around five o'clock the gate would open and he would come out to take the dogs for a walk. He knows something, I said to myself. He's either super-enlightened or incredibly stoned, but whatever it is, he's keeping some sort of a spiritual secret and I'm going to get to the bottom of it!

Robin, meanwhile, was no help at all. "Don't you notice anything strange about living here?" I asked him one day as he stood glaring off into the distance.

"Aye, I cannae paint a damn thing. It's too perfect. It doesnae inspire me. You cannae improve on nature so why try. I prefer the Glasgow tenaments...dirty, noisy, decaying buildings with a lot of character. Everything is so bloody intense over here. The peace is intense. The sun is intense. The rain storms bring down landslides. The cliffs are too steep and the oceans too violent. They tell you it's God's country; but to me it's a hostile environment. The mist in Scotland sweeps down the glens so gently. This damn fog is like a pillow trying to suffocate you."

"Yeah, well, your gentle Scottish mist swept down the glen into my California lungs and mildewed them so badly that I had pneumonia once and bronchitis about a hundred percent of the time I lived there, so give me the intense sun any day!"

He was quiet for awhile and then he said, "My dad would like it here. He likes the sea."

I remembered when I had met Robin in art school in Glasgow. He had insisted on taking me to visit his father's home town in Fife. We'd ridden for miles on a bus through little gray stone villages, past moors and locks, until we'd come to the coast and the little town of East Weems.

There had been a mining disaster some while back so the town was dead and the people in it were as good as ghosts. The men sat all day beside the sea wall, collecting unemployment and staring off into space. Robin's father had looked at me, a foreigner, and known that his son would go off to America and raise a family that he would never know and could never afford to come and visit.

And now we were in Big Sur and Robin was holding the baby and brooding over the fog, having a private consultation with the old miners of Fife, a million miles away.

I hated to bother him when he was in this mood, but I really needed to know. "It's just that I keep getting this feeling...like I'm an intruder or something...back up there on the hillside. It's like there are shadows, and I hear whispering. I wondered if you had felt anything like that at all?"

"There's a right daft chap across the way at Valentine's place," Robin replied. "He looks like a bloomin' sleepwalker. Why don't you ask him about it. Jamie and I are away for a nap."

That evening I worked later than usual in the driveway, pruning ceanothus, and poking nasturtium seeds into the wine-barrel planter, hoping to speak to the eccentric dog walker. Sure enough the gate opened at five o'clock and out limped Booger, the fat old black German shepherd, followed by a bouncy young blond collie, and behind them came the caretaker.

"It's a beautiful evening," I called out to him.

He turned very slowly and looked at me, or possibly, through me, as if I were some unexpected apparition.

"They are all beautiful," he said, without expression.

"So they are!" I agreed, cheerfully. "We are so lucky to live here in paradise."

He stared at me again for a moment and then replied, "Paradise is in your head." And turning he made his way off down the road after the dogs, his white muslin shirt blowing in the evening breeze like a sailboat cruising silently off into another dimension.

"Damn!" I said. "It's a conspiracy. I know it is!"

Several days later I had the occasion to meet another one of our neighbors. There had been a freak summer shower that morning and the mist had lifted at last, leaving the hillside freshly rinsed and shining. Robin was rushing off to try a painting and I had hoisted Jamie into the backpack carrier to hike down to the highway and meet the mail truck.

The mailboxes for the residents of Partington Ridge stood in a multicolored line at the foot of the hill on the ocean side of the highway. Behind them was an old wooden plank bench where the locals could sit and socialize while waiting for news from the outside world. It was on this bench that I met the Billygoat Man. I had seen him striding up and down the road from time to time, and it was because of his long side whiskers and goatee that I had given him the nickname.

Unlike my glassy-eyed neighbor, this man always seemed cheerful and alert, giving me a wave whenever I passed. Today he came winding down the ridge road in his little blue VW bug as I sat watching the steam evaporate off the redwood trees in Partington Canyon. Just as he emerged from his car a fantastic rainbow appeared, linking both the north and south ridge together in an arc of colors.

"Isn't that a lovely sight?" I called to him.

"She's a beauty, all right," he replied. "One of my private stock. Polychrome IV, I call her. I just hung her out a minute ago. They mold if they're kept in storage too long."

While I was digesting this bit of information, Jamie decided to reach out his little hand and yank on the Billygoat Man's whiskers.

"Good God!" the man shouted, jumping back in alarm. "There's some sort of a beastie in your backpack!"

It was at this point that the mailman arrived, and I introduced myself, explaining that we were caretaking the Maud Oakes' house which had recently been purchased by her niece.

"Where the hell did Maud go off to this time?" asked the Billygoat Man.

"South America, I believe. To study some primitive Indian civilization. She's an anthropologist, I think."

"Yes, indeed," said the Billygoat Man. "She's a wonderful womaness! My name's Bob. Would you care for a ride back up the hill?"

I agreed thankfully, as I was not relishing the thought of climbing back up the ridge with the heavy baby on my back. He gave me his mail to hold and as we wound our way up the road, I glanced down at the envelopes and found that they were addressed to Bob and Rosa Nash. Either the Billygoat man had a "womaness" of his own or Rosa was another one of his private rainbows.

My question was answered as we rounded a corner and he pointed to where the rainbow had been. "She's gone now," he said. "My wife must have taken her in. They fade if you leave them out in the sun too long."

This man was definitely strange, but at least he was talkative and

I decided to confide in him. "There is something strange about Maud's place," I said. "It's kind of spooky. I feel like I'm being watched by dark shadows."

Mr. Nash stopped the car in the middle of the road and turned to me very seriously, looking directly into my eyes.

"It's the Indians," he said. "The whole damn place is built on an old shell mound and they don't take kindly to desecration. Jesus, Maud had a hell of a time with that first house of hers. It was up the hill from where you live…up a little path, and over on the flat spot where you get the lovely view to the north. But they burned it down. The Indian spirits didn't want it there so they just got rid of it.

"She built the new house lower down on the property, but things weren't much better. When she'd want to write or do any serious thinking she'd have to go round with a candle and a stick of incense and tell the buggers to get the hell out and leave her alone.

"Alan Watts used to come and stay there a lot, too. He's another heavy vibration that could be hanging around the place. You'll have to make your own peace with them. They just don't take kindly to newcomers. You may have to burn some sage or make a few sacrifices. Take that beastie of yours, for instance. He's just about the right size for a barbecue."

At this point I thanked Mr. Nash and bailed out at the fork in the road, thanking him for his help.

"You'll have to come by and visit us one of these days," he invited. "Up the hill and first road on the left. We live in a greenhouse. Well, it's not actually a greenhouse yet. It hasn't been built yet, but it will be someday. Right now it's only a tarp."

I started off down the road, my head spinning with all this mysterious new information. People who lived under a tarp and hung rainbows out to dry, shell mounds, Indian spirits, dead philosophers, and sacrifices. What sort of metaphysical mumbo jumbo was going on here?

From Harrydick's library I borrowed Lillian Boss Ross's *The Stranger*, Henry Miller's *Oranges of Hieronymus Bosch*, and several books of Robertson Jeffer's poems and I discovered that I was not alone. This strange, timeless, cosmic aura that surrounded Big Sur seemed to be common knowledge to anyone who had lived there for any length of time. But how did one learn to co-exist peacefully with it? I turned next to some Indian writings and took careful notes.

"Nearness to nature keeps the spirit sensitive to impressions not commonly felt, and in touch with unseen powers. To sit or lie upon the ground, the mother earth, is to be able to think more deeply and feel more keenly. There is only one life duty and that is the daily recognition of the unseen and the eternal. Each soul must face the advancing dawn, the new sweet earth and the great silence alone. Before you can talk to the holy ones you must meditate, purify, and prepare yourself and your offerings. Then you may fill your peace pipe and offer it to the sky and the earth and the water. Then you can smoke together, and they will be ready to talk."

And so for weeks I prepared myself, feeling the same sort of excitement and expectation that I might feel if I were getting ready for a wedding day or meeting a long lost brother or sister for the first time.

At last I felt that I was ready. I filled Robin's pipe with tobacco the night before, and hid it under my side of the bed for the next morning. I planned to sneak out before dawn and climb the path to my ley-line spot. I would know it, even in the dark because it would be warm under my feet.

The next morning I woke at four o'clock as if someone had tapped me on the shoulder. Everyone was asleep. My husband, the baby, the cat. Nobody would miss me for awhile. I had thought I might need a flashlight, but the moon was full, lighting up the ocean like a football stadium, so I just grabbed my peace pipe and ran out the door in my nightgown.

I ran up the hillside, slipping on pine needles and repeating a Tewa Indian chant to myself over and over again so I wouldn't lose courage.

DRINKING TO KINDNESS

> "Yonder comes the dawn
> The Universe grows green
> The road to the underworld is open!
> Yet now we live
> Upward going, upward going!"

"Upward going, upward going," I kept saying to myself, as I climbed the hill. "The road to the underworld is open...all road blocks are down...here I come spirits...upward going...upward going."

I finally arrived and sat on the topmost spot, under the big eucalyptus tree that stood among the pines. The dawn was turning all pink and purple and the sun was just about to explode over the top of the Santa Lucias. I had known exactly what I was going to say. I'd written it down and memorized it like the 23rd Psalm in Sunday School, but suddenly I was flustered and flooded with emotion and my words came out all cock-eyed and stupid and not at all like I'd planned.

"Hey!" I shouted to the morning world. "It's me, Kristin, and I've brought a peace pipe!

I want to be part of you.

Ocean spirits, sky spirits, redwood spirits,

Seagulls, bluejays, hummingbirds and hawks,

Raccoons, rock cod, whales, bobcats, and sea otters,

Ghost of philosophers, wise men and shamans,

I am your sister, I am your friend,

And I count, too, so don't hang so heavy over my head!

Sit down here with me at sunrise,

And smoke a little peace pipe, damnit!"

Suddenly the sun came up and the sea began to quiver with the first wave of morning, and the birds woke up, and the trees woke up, and I began to dance, swaying the way the eucalyptus trees were showing me.

"That's right, that's right," they nodded, "but don't hold your branches so close to your trunk. Look, swing them around the way we do."

"Why haven't you spoken to me before?" I called to them breathlessly as I danced in the breeze.

The trees shook their heads and moaned. "Oh, we've spoken. We've broken our branches waving to you; we've shaken ourselves sore singing to you in the storms, but you never noticed. We are out here every morning to greet the dawn and dance while you're sleeping. Don't you know we are all the earth's children? We are all made of the same material and we are all one energy. Our roots are in the ground you stand on; our green leaves fill your lungs with air, and the whales' lungs, and the seagulls...you're eating food from the same ocean they do and collecting salt and mussels off the same rocks as the Indians, and the bones of those Indians are in the very soil you stand on. Sing her the song, Bones. Sing her the song of the earth spirit."

And from somewhere deep in the ground came the hollow, clattering voice of the ancient Indian bones.

> "I, I am the spirit within the earth
> The feet of the earth are my feet
> The legs of the earth are my legs
> The bodily strength of the earth is my bodily strength
> The thoughts of the earth are my thoughts
> The voice of the earth is my voice
> All that belongs to the sacred earth, belongs to me
> I, I am the sacred earth."

All the time that the bones were chanting, the light of the new day was creeping into every corner of the coastline, and then somewhere down Partington Ridge I heard a car starting up.

It was like a sound from another world...the world that only an hour ago was the only one I knew existed. But now things would be different. Now I was an interloper. Like learning to play a violin or discovering I could suddenly speak Swahili, I had conquered a new dimension!

V
Paradise Lost

As it turned out, the end of summer came and went, and still by December Keeker did not feel up to the the challenge of life in Big Sur, so our caretaking duties were extending through the New Year. We had been there approximately six months attempting to live on the $100 a month that we received to house sit. We lived mostly on macaroni, top Ramen noodles, potato soup and the government handouts that the Health Department program provided for me and the baby. Cereal, cornmeal, dried beans and milk.

Robin was fairly oblivious to it, being deeply engrossed in his never-ending struggle as the angry young artist, but I was becoming more and more depressed. I planted a little vegetable garden, hoping that, like the magical Findhorn Garden in Scotland, this sandy soil that lacked all the proper nutrients, would burst forth with oversized carrots, onions, green beans and tomatoes, but it didn't.

With some help from my mother we had managed to acquire a little VW bug for $200, that you had to roll down the hill to pop start. This was, of course, no great problem since Partington Ridge was practically all vertical, but since my husband didn't drive, I was the one who had to travel the thirty miles into Monterey for food. On rare occasions I would even treat myself to the luxury of visiting the laundromat with our clothes and baby diapers, rather than trying to stuff them into the bathroom sink at home.

Harrydick was concerned about us. There was an art gallery not far from Partington Ridge and he urged me to take Robin's work and see if they'd show it.

"They've had a hell of a time," he told me of the owners. "First year Gary bought it he was hit with a landslide that destroyed the place and closed down the highway for months, but they've rebuilt now with some old redwood water tanks and I think business is starting to pick up again. It's worth a try anyway, and you tell Gary I sent you down."

So I packed up Robin's abstract landscapes and dream visions that he had been stock piling for a one-man show in San Francisco, or New York, or Paris...the ones that were going to someday make us rich, and I headed for the Coast Gallery.

The work was not what the average tourist would be looking for. No sunsets of lighthouses or seals on a windswept rock. The largest painting was about half the size of me and it depicted the heads of Shakespearian actors inside various-sized bottles and jars. It was titled, "The Actor's Jungle Survival Kit." Another one, about the same size, had been done on a cold and foggy day when the artist was brooding about having nothing else to draw, and it featured a colorful heaps of toys, a fire engine, a rubberducky, some tennis shoes and a pacifier.

I took some of the new etchings from the artists' workshop and an impressive sounding biography which I had typed up. I figured that at least it would get me in the front door, and if they didn't like the work, perhaps they might need some help at the counter for the holiday season.

As I wound my way down the ridge I went over again the information that Harrydick had given me about the proprietors. Gary had been an English teacher in Oregon who had dropped out and become a candle maker, working in his VW bus as he went from one Renaissance fair to another.

Finally he had spent all of his money to buy the old Coast Gallery, only to have it destroyed in a landslide. He had recently married Vicki, a girl much younger than himself, and together with the help of the goodhearted locals, they had set about rebuilding the place, using two huge water tanks which Gary bought cheap from the City of Oakland water company when they updated their equipment. The highway was open again and the imposing facade of the great tanks drew the attention of curious tourists who made a special point of stopping to visit this novel-looking structure.

I assumed that they opened at nine o'clock so I had made a point of getting there bright and early before the highway got busy. The sign on the front of the tank still said CLOSED but the big wooden door was open a crack so I ventured on inside. It was very dark in the huge redwood room as there were no windows, but there was light shining through the isinglass on a big old-fashioned wood stove. I could just make out the eerie shapes of twisted burl lamps, marble sculptures, and bronze mobiles bobbing from the ceiling.

As I was making my way slowly to the counter a man suddenly appeared through a little side door. He was wearing an Irish tweed Donegal hat, a pin-striped suit jacket and boxer shorts. I felt rather embarrassed, having sneaked in, and I turned to leave, quickly muttering an apology as I went.

"No, no, no, come on in. It's OK. Just pretend I'm in a bathing suit," the man called to me. "See, my slacks are right here…25 cents at the Goodwill, and I've got two more pairs just like them. And this nice jacket….it was 50 cents. My wife tried to talk them down, but they wouldn't budge. The only thing wrong with these pants is that the zipper is broken. I brought a needle and thread, and I was going to try and mend them before we opened, but you caught me…with my pants down, so to speak!" he laughed. "Spring's the name. Bill Spring."

I introduced myself and told him I lived up on Partington and that Harrydick had sent me down.

"Good, good," he said handing me the pants and the needle and thread. "You work on this zipper and I'll get the lights on and the coffee made."

Bill began dashing around, inside and out, filling a large coffee maker from a garden hose out on the patio, lighting candles, and turning on manzanita burl lamps while I fumbled with the 25-cent bargain trousers.

Somehow I managed to get the zipper back on track and Bill had just slipped into them, when another person came storming in the front door, head down, muttering to himself.

"Ah, good morning, Larry!" Bill called cheerfully.

The person named Larry did not reply but went straight to the coffee pot, heaping his cup full of powdered creamer and three spoonfuls of sugar. He appeared to be a nice-looking, sandy-haired fellow in his mid-thirties with a big drooping mustache.

"Rough night, eh?" Bill said, giving me a wink.

"I've had it, Bill," Larry said. "I mean it this time. I can't take anymore. She's so crazy! Throughly nuts...loony tunes...insane. Jesus, just wait 'til you hear this. I get home last night. I'm tired, right? I've been pouring cylinder candles all day...really cranking 'em out...and waiting on crazy customers, right?

"I just want to go home at the end of the day...relax, eat a little dinner...I'm looking forward to a nice little goddamn peaceful evening. So what happens? I get home and my trailer is full of slimeballs. You wouldn't believe these guys...the dregs...hitchhikers from under every bridge on the coast...I don't know where she finds them, but she does. And not just hitchhikers, but their dogs, too. Mangy, fleabag dogs, with little bleeding paws are lying all over my bed. MY BED! And these assholes are sitting in MY house, smoking MY dope, in MY chair, making themselves right at fucking home.

"Who pays the rent and buys the goddamn food? I DO. I'm telling you, Bill, she's going to have to take her sleazybag boyfriends and get the hell out because I've had it!" And with that, Larry stormed out the side door and off to the candle shop to take out his revenge on the wax vat.

Bill laughed and shook his head. "Poor Larry. He has more trouble with that girlfriend of his. Do you know Louise? No? Well, she's a nut. When they first started going together she came to the Gallery and offered her services as a stream cleaner. Gary tried to be nice to her because she was Larry's girlfriend and so he asked her what a stream cleaner did and if it was something she thought he needed.

"She led him over to Lafler Creek which runs down the canyon in back of the candle shop and pointed out all sorts of improvements that needed to be made, such as rocks moved, banks stabilized by proper planting...things only a stream cleaner would know about, and so Gary took her up on it.

"A week later she had ripped out all of Vicki's carefully cultivated watercress, changed the course of the creek and left the Gallery gardening tools in the stream itself. This did not make her too popular with the management. Still, love is blind, and even when she brought home a rooster and two chickens and insisted they live inside the trailer because otherwise they might get attacked by raccoons, Larry let her have her way."

"So today's outburst was nothing unusual?" I asked.

"No, no," Bill laughed. "By the end of the day Larry will be telling you what an interesting bunch of guys those hitchhikers were and what a good judge of character she is."

Suddenly from out on the highway there came a loud screeching of tires and then the hiss of air brakes.

"Here we go," said Bill. "First tour bus of the day. We'd better warn Larry." He picked up the phone and gave the intercom a buzz. "Front and center, Dr. Wax," he said. "We have a large load of hitchhikers pulling in. I believe they're headed for your trailer." Bill winked. "That got him," he laughed.

I could hardly believe the way the room was filling up. They were swarming in through the door like honeybees, couples of all shapes and sizes with New York accents and Florida baggage tags on their camera cases.

The first woman in the door headed straight for me. "Where's the little girl's room, honey?" she whispered.

"Give her the key." Bill gestured to something that looked like a petrified buzzard claw hanging behind the cash register. I hesitated and then reluctantly picked the thing up and saw that attached to it on a little leather thong was a small brass key.

The woman pulled her hand back in horror as I passed it to her.

"It's a manzanita burl, madam," Bill explained. "Just so we don't lose it. Go out the door to the patio and make a sharp left. The door says W.C."

The woman studied it for a moment and then took it reluctantly, holding it at arm's length, and calling to a long line of ladies to fall in behind her. She didn't quite make it out the door before her husband spotted her. "What the hell are you buying now, Mildred?" he yelled. "Jesus, we've only been in here three minutes and she's at it already."

The arrival of the tour bus had roused Vicki, who came dashing down from the apartment above the candle shop looking not quite awake, to see if Bill needed any help. She was surprised to find me there behind the counter, but before I could explain, the husband of the woman who had gone off to the little girl's room, came up and grabbed my arm. "Where's your film, Miss?" he said. "You sell film, don't you?"

I looked over at Vicki who shook her head. "Sorry, we don't."

"Well, just come outside with me a minute, Miss," he said, still holding on to my arm. "I just want you to show me something."

I allowed myself to be led through the crowd and out the front door where we stood on the front steps of the gallery watching the mist blow around on the ocean below.

"Tell me where the Big Sur is?" he asked, waving his free hand around to take in all the surroundings. "It's a rock or something, right? Is it around here someplace? I wanta get a picture of it."

"Sur means south in Spanish," I explained. "Monterey used to be the old Spanish capitol and everything south of there was El Grande de la Sur; the great land to the south. Big Sur is this whole area, this beautiful long stretch of coastline."

"It's not a rock?" he asked sadly.

"I'm afraid not, but you could photograph any number of scenic spots around here and it would be the Big Sur."

"Is that a fact?" he said gloomily. "So what time does this fog lift?"

"Well, sometimes it's gone by noon, and sometimes it stays all day. You never can tell."

The little man shook his head and released the grip he had on my arm, turning to go back into the Gallery. "Mildred!" he shouted. "It's not a rock! Where da hell did she get to anyway?"

When I got back to the counter Bill was busy selling a redwood key chain and Vicki was talking to a woman who was covered in ivory jewelry.

"I'm in love with your hippo!" the woman cooed. "My husband likes the giraffe, but he knows once I see a hippo there's no contest. I'm a hippo maniac!"

Vicki was nodding her head eagerly, causing her very long brown hair, which was tied back in a ponytail, to swish up and down on her bottom like a feather duster, brushing off the seat of her pants.

"If you're traveling, a hippo is your best bet," Vicki said. "It's so much easier to travel with a hippo than with a giraffe. Because of the neck, you know. The one that really gives us trouble is the horse. He's so difficult to ship because his leg is sticking out." She stuck out her hand as if she were a filly in mid prance.

"Well, I think that pelican takes the prize," another woman piped up. "My son lives on the cape and I can just see that pelican sitting in the bay window, gazing off to sea."

"Time to saddle up, ladies and gentlemen!" called the tour bus driver.

"Ooooooh, what am I going to do?" wailed the ivory woman. "Betty! Betty! Come over here and give me some advice. I've fallen in love with a hippo."

"What on earth are they talking about?" I whispered to Bill.

"The Loet Vanderveen sculptures, upstairs," he whispered back. "Yes, madam, can I help you?"

A plump, red-faced lady was hurriedly handing Bill a stuffed sea otter. "He's so PRECIOUS!" she cried. "Is it real fur?"

"No, madam, we are trying to preserve the wildlife here, not destroy it," he replied.

"Well, he looks *so* real," she said, giving the otter a last pat. "Don't wrap him up too tightly. I don't want him to suffocate."

When the hippo had been purchased, and the otters and candles and keyring were packaged, and the bathroom key returned, the bus party departed, and we all sat back to recover.

It was at this point that Gary came striding in, freshly showered and splendidly turned out in a puff-sleeved paisley Renaissance shirt, his red beard neatly combined and his multi-colored beret tilted at a jaunty angle. He was somewhat perturbed to find that the coffee pot was empty.

"What's the problem here?" he said.

"We had a tour bus," Bill explained.

"And I sold a hundred-and-eighty-dollar hippo!" Vicki said defiantly.

"And I fixed Bill's fly," I piped up.

Gary and Vicki both looked at me in astonishment.

"I live up on Partington Ridge," I explained. "My husband's an artist and Harrydick wanted me to come down and show you his work. We're getting kind of low on money and I thought you might need some help around here, but when I arrived…well, Bill had no pants on because of his fly."

"You aren't a stream cleaner, are you?" Gary asked suspiciously.

"No, no. I stay away from that sort of thing."

"Well, OK. We don't have any zippers that need fixing, but go ahead and bring in the paintings and I'll take a look at them. It will have to be consignment, you know. We don't have enough money to buy right now. And then maybe you could help Vicki unpack a load of stoneware pottery in the back room. I'd like to get it out before the next bus load arrives."

I ran out to the Volkswagen bug filled with hope and anticipation. I hadn't really wanted a job. The magical world on top of the ridge had become so hypnotically peaceful, but living on our $100-a-month caretaker's allowance was a definite strain. Having more money would certainly be a welcome change. In an odd way it was sort of refreshing to be out in the real world again.

Perhaps Valentine's caretaker had been right and paradise was only in your head, but what the heck. If a woman from Miami could fall in love with a hundred-and-eighty-dollar hippo, then surely someone, somewhere, must be desperately in need of an Actor's Jungle Survival Kit.

VI
Trouble Shooting

Bill and Larry and I proved to be a pretty good team. More and more Gary and Vicki would leave us alone at the cash desk, which was known as "Control." Gary had decided to pursue his old journalistic talents by creating a local newspaper, mostly to spread the word that the government was trying to take over the Big Sur coast and turn it into a national park.

This prospect had the old ranchers and homestead families up in arms, while the newcomer environmentalists insisted it was a good idea to maintain the beauty of the coastline by forbidding anyone else to built there and make the place into a sort of shrine. Town meetings were held and the once harmonious residents of the wilderness took emotional sides on the issue.

While Gary was becoming submerged in local politics, Vicki had her hands full with the gallery bookkeeping, of which there was getting to be more and more of as business picked up and the number of artists and craftsmen increased.

Bill and I had been given the titles of "Anchorman" and "Troubleshooter" and Larry had been promoted from "Candle Elf" to "Head Candlemaker," since Gary was now far too busy for the wax vats. I think his theory was that since he could not afford to raise our salaries, he would give us all titles instead to make us feel more important. It was no easy task for my little family to live on my $3.50 an hour part-time job, but with Robin's art selling so slowly, I felt lucky to have it and besides I was getting to meet a lot of interesting people.

One of the regulars was Walter Trotter, who only came in for the coffee. Walter was to Big Sur what Paul Bunyon was to the Redwood Country. First there was Sam Trotter, who came here from Missouri in the 1800s. He was a big, grizzly, hard-working man with a lot of dubious legends attached to him. His sons had grown up to be just as big, and they were now the "main men" in Big Sur. Whether you wanted a house built, or a landslide moved, or a wild boar shot, or a sink unplugged, you called a Trotter.

I had never met any of them up until this time, and although I had heard that Walter only lived about a half-mile from the Gallery, I had never imagined that a man who was rumored to shoot trespassers and kill rattlesnakes by picking them up and snapping their heads off, would be the type to stop by for some art appreciation.

As I remember, we had just gotten in a shipment of silly little wooden sea gulls which sat on miniature wooden pilings, buoys and rocks, and I had been given the job of arranging them into the kind of eye catching, souvenir display that no tourist would want to go home without. Neither Gary nor Vicki would admit to having ordered them, and after unpacking the box they had both stared at the contents in alarm and then hurried off to do other things.

Bill was just suggesting we make them more lifelike by sprinkling guano around on the display shelf, when a dark shadow blocked the sun coming through the front door, and a voice like thunder growled, "What the hell is that crap supposed to be?"

I was terrified to turn around, but Bill's face lit up as cheerfully as always, and he said, "This is ART, Walter. You oughta buy one. They're only fifteen bucks apiece."

Walter lumbered over and pick up one of the seagulls. His hands were like baseball mitts, but surprisingly he held the tiny sculpture very delicately. "Jeeezzus," he said, setting it back down again. "This stuff ain't worth shit."

I was just about to giggle, when suddenly he turned and addressed me in the same thundering voice he had entered with. "Your pansy-assed husband just telephoned me and ordered some firewood for that woman that bought Maud Oakes' place," he boomed. "Said I should come here and get directions from you. Why the hell does he let you go out and work while he stays home to babysit? Must have his head up his butt."

I had, of course, wondered the same thing about a hundred times myself, but for some reason I felt a little defensive about being attacked by this bullying giant.

"He's an ARTIST, Walter," Bill explained. "He's very original. You should go upstairs and have a look at his work."

Oh, God, no, I thought. *If he thought the seagulls were crap, I didn't want to know what his opinion of Robin's abstract watercolors and the pickled heads of Shakespearian actors would be.* But Walter did as he was told, and he was gone for a long time. I held my breath while dusting displays and polishing glass sculpture cases.

Just as he was clumping back down the stairs, Gary and Vicki appeared in the doorway all dressed up and ready to go off to Monterey for their "town day."

"Well, well, if it isn't himself," cried Gary. "Don't tell me you've decided to put a little bit of culture into your life."

"Watch your fucking tongue, asshole," Walter snapped. "I was upstairs looking at this Robin Coventry guy's stuff. He's weird, but he can draw. You oughta get him to sketch some of my Dad's old homesteads while they're still standing."

And so it turned out that this man I had been prepared to hate became our lifesaver, and Robin began getting commissions to draw the old landmarks, cabins and barns, up and down the coast.

When Gary and Vicki went off to town they would leave us with their old gray guard dog, Shadow, and a long list of projects, just in case we thought their absence might be our cue to kick back and put our feet up. Number one on the list was always, "Touch everything with love."

DRINKING TO KINDNESS

Today, the list they had left was particularly long:

- Take down all stained glass windws, wash them and hang them in a new display.
- Dust and wax redwood and manzanita sculptures and lamps.
- Paintings need faces washed.
- Black widow patrol on outdoor items: birdhouses, planters, and wind chimes.
- Make a new sign for W.C. - "COUNTRY JOHNS ARE NOT LIKE TOWN NOTHING EXTRA WILL GO DOWN"

"Seems like they left us with a lot of big projects today," I said to Bill. "Do you think we'll have time to wait on customers?"

"Don't worry about it," said Bill who was hauling the huge black leather briefcase that he brought to work every day up onto the counter. "They just feel guilty about going away and leaving us with nothing to do. Why don't you run upstairs to the apartment and get us all a nice cold glass of tonic water."

"Tonic water?" I said.

"It's a little too early for the gin yet. Go get Larry to show you where they keep it. I've got work to do."

Larry was only too happy to join me on a raid of the apartment. I explained that Bill had asked for tonic water and said he had a lot of work to do. "That big heavy briefcase of his," I said, "what's in it? Does he do the ordering or something?"

Larry laughed. "Those are Bill's racing forms. He goes to the horse races up in San Francisco every weekend. That briefcase is full of research...it's like a science to him, and he takes it very seriously, but his wife will never let him bet more than five dollars."

Upstairs in the apartment there were cats everywhere and the smell of Shadow's eczema was fierce. The cats were curled up in heaps like hibernating snakes, and the place was sort of dark and spooky. Larry, however, seemed right at home, filling the cups with ice and tonic and poking around in the cupboards, commenting that the crackers were stale and the cheese was moldy. Apparently this was all part of the town day routine.

I left Larry and Bill chatting over the racing forms with their cocktails and took my own drink into the other room along with a hammer and nails to tackle the job of washing and rearranging the stained glass windows.

I was doing pretty well, becoming more confident and admiring my new display when it happened. One of the nails I was hammering in was too close to the window frame. It penetrated the edge of the plate glass window inside, creating a huge series of spiderweb-like cracks shooting out from the top of the floor-length pane. I could only stand and stare, horrified at what I'd done.

Suddenly, as I looked at the window I realized there was someone outside staring back at me. Deep blue eyes, a mop of brown curly hair and an ethereal elfish grin. I would have taken him for Pan except that he held a shovel instead of pipes, and was leaning against a wheelbarrel full of pine needles.

"Beautiful!" he called through the crack. "Like a giant snowflake. A great improvement."

I burst into tears and ran back to Control to tell Bill.

"I broke a goddam window...I didn't mean to...I put a nail through the frame and it made a big, huge crack, and now they're gonna kill me, and I'll be fired, and I don't have any money to pay for the damage...what will I do?" I bubbled away.

Bill began calmly folding his racing forms and replacing them back in the briefcase. "I'm sure it's nothing to worry about," he said. "Let's go have a look."

As we were viewing the disaster, the mysterious blue-eyed stranger, who had been behind the snowflake, came strolling into the room.

"Hello, Alan," said Bill. "What do you think? If we just hang a big, colorful stained-glass window in front of it nobody will ever notice."

"I like it," said the person named Alan.

"Let's have another round of tonic water," Bill suggested, so, sniffling, I went off to get more tonic water, stopping at the candle shop to tell Larry what I had done.

"Outrageous! Wonderful!" Larry cried happily. "Last week I was dusting a glass shelf full of candle holders and the shelf cracked and all the candle holders fell down and broke. It was an accident...happens all the time. Don't worry about it."

"There's some spacey guy down there named Alan who thinks it looks better than it did before," I said.

"Oh, my God, not Alan," said Larry. "He's such a trip. He does the gardening around here sometimes for a little pocket change. He lives in a tent down in Partington Canyon. I've known him for years. We go way back to the old Haight Ashbury days in San Francisco when I was known as Ark, the Flutemaker, selling my wares on the street corner.

"One time Alan decided he'd like to see what the Golden Gate Bridge looked like from the top of the towers, so he climbed right up to the top. They had to stop traffic and close the bridge down to get him off.

"Then, another time, he jumped off the cliff out there on the point to see what it was like to fly. He had planned on landing on a little ledge halfway down, but he missed it and just went sailing right on down. His mom was sitting home in Santa Cruz in her little trailer park watching TV when she saw the cops hauling some madman up out of the ocean, and she recognized him. The last time she had watched the news was when they had to stop the traffic on the Golden Gate Bridge, so now she won't watch the news anymore because she's afraid of what she might see."

I was about to ask more about this crazy Alan guy when I heard the hiss of the air brakes as a bus party pulled in. Just as I was running past the lower room where the stained glass windows were waiting for me, I saw the bus backing up to park closer in toward the building. As he did, the top of the big vehicle grazed the edge of the outside rafter above my broken window. The force of the bump caused my single snowflake to be transformed into a massive blizzard.

The cracking sound brought Bill and Alan hurrying back into the room again. "Wow!" said Alan. "It looked like such a nice day out today, who would have guessed we were in for a snowstorm."

Bill laughed and happily slapped me on the back. "Ha!" he said. "You see how things work out. Now the bus company will have to buy Gary a new window. They have plenty of insurance. Everything will be taken care of. I told you it would be all right. You worry too much."

VII
Will the Real Miss Woods Please Stand Up

Every afternoon at one o'clock, rain or shine, tour bus or not, as soon as Bill had finished his lunch, a toasted cheddar-cheese-and-green-pepper sandwich, he would call his wife, Barbara, and report on how the day was going. Even though they had been married for something like thirty years, these conversations always struck me as very romantic, since Bill's voice seemed rather hushed and giggly. That is, until the day Barbara chopped down the deodar tree.

"So what are you up to?" Bill had asked, after complimenting the cheddar cheese and green pepper sandwich, and reporting on the number of sales we'd made. "You WHAT! You *are* kidding aren't you? But you couldn't have...that tree is huge...I LIKED that tree...Barbara, I don't believe this!"

After he hung up he looked at me and shook his head. "She cut down my deodar tree," he said miserably. "Never trust a woman with a chainsaw in her hand."

Several weeks later I got to meet Bill's wife as she was passing by the gallery, returning from a town trip. She had stopped to show

Bill the latest treasures she had found at the Goodwill store. A new blue shirt, a pair of pants with a working zipper and several blouses for herself, all under a dollar.

Barbara was an auburn-haired, solid-looking woman, with a warm smile and a heavy English accent. I asked how the two of them had met, explaining to her that I was married to a Scotsman and had lived in the U.K. for a number of years.

"She's my war bride," Bill beamed. "She's a sculptor, you know. You must come over sometime and see our house. She does wonderful work."

"Yes, please do," Barbara agreed. "Come and have a cup of tea. We're just down at Burns Creek. Bill will tell you the way."

"She was quite right about the deodar tree, by the way," Bill said seriously. "The patio looks far better without it."

There was something comforting about a nice, sensible English lady, and a good cup of tea that I had been missing living among all these crazy Big Sur folk. I decided I would try to go visit Barbara on my next day off. Bill gave me directions and told me to go around to the back of the house where Barbara would be working in her studio.

On Friday, I set out for Burns Creek and found the house quite easily. It was just as Bill had said. Barbara was around the back bent over the headless wooden body of a neatly dressed woman holding a handbag.

"Poor Miss Woods," said Barbara, giving her sculpture a loving pat. "She's had a nasty fall, and lost her head."

Outside the workshop door a pair of legs stood upside down, tennis shoes in the air. "Do you think it will rain?" Barbara asked, glancing up at the darkening sky, "Or can we just leave her legs out while we have a cup of tea?"

In the house, Barbara busied herself putting the kettle on and stoking up the wood stove while I wandered about the dimly lit room, not quite sure what was real and what was not.

After a year in Big Sur, I should have known better than to expect the Spring's house to have the sort of proper Presbyterian sitting room that I had so often encountered in Britain; somehow her accent had suggested it, but what I was seeing was even more amazing than anything I had yet come across in any Big Sur home.

A man playing a cello, peeked at us from an upstairs loft. A shelf of what turned out to be wooden books, held a plate of wooden hors d'oeuvres, while hooks above the kitchen counter held big wooden cuts of meat and wooden frying pans.

"Here we are then," said Barbara, setting a tray of teacups and cookies beside the couch. I peered at it suspiciously, half expecting the whole thing to be another wooden sculpture.

"Tell me about this stuff," I said. "Tell me how you and Bill got together and how you started doing these things."

"Well, I was raised on the coast of Wales. It was a wild place, very like Big Sur, and then, when I was ten, my father died and we moved back to Kent where my mother started a poultry farm. We had no electricity, no car, no anything. Eventually I started going to art school. I was a painter at first, but then one day I found a piece of clay. It was just regular old clay out of the ground, but I started working with it and soon switched all my studies to sculpture."

Barbara topped off my tea cup and then went on with the story. "When World War Two broke out, I joined the WAAFS and that's how Bill and I met. I was working on radar in the Air Force and he was in that cloak and dagger thing…the OSS, or whatever you call it. I went to art school in the evenings and sometimes I'd have to walk five miles back home in a blackout.

"Well, anyway, Bill and I were married and I gave up art. Didn't touch it again for ten years. The night our daughter, Cynthia, was born there was an air raid that knocked out part of our house. Our other girl, Frances, came next and she was born early because the goat butted me. Goat induction you might call it," she laughed and paused to munch on a cookie. "Am I boring you?" she asked.

"Not at all. This is fascinating," I replied.

"Well, let's see. When the war was over we moved to the States and lived in Rochester, New York, in an old abandoned farm house on the shores of Lake Ontario. The kids must have been about six or seven then. The place was so filthy that we couldn't eat inside so we cooked out over a camp fire. Cynthia fell in the fire once and had a terrible scar for years. Then I was berry picking one day to make us a little money and Frances got her foot run over by a tractor. Oh, God, what we went through. More tea?"

I had been so engrossed in the story that I had forgotten all about the tea, so I gulped it down and held my cup out for more. "How in the world did you ever end up in Big Sur?" I asked.

"Well, one morning Bill came in. He was shaving at the time and he said, 'How would you like to go to California?' I have no idea what brought that on, but I said, 'When do we leave?'

"We crossed the country in an ancient Oldsmobile. The kids had their feet hanging out the windows because it was so hot. When we got to California we had no job, no house and no money. We stayed in an old trailer and then in a boarding house. Finally we put an ad in the paper and someone offered us a house. She is still our friend today. I got a job teaching art and Bill got a little electrician's hifi shop.

"Our next door neighbor was Charlie Levitsky's sister. Do you know Charlie and Melissa? They live over in Coastlands, across from Ventana. Well, anyway, it was through him that we started coming down to Big Sur. We rented the old hospital building at Anderson Canyon for $12.50 a month. That was the place where they used to treat the Chinese laborers when the highway was being built.

"It turned out I knew a lot of the people in Bug Sur through the art world. Later we met Boris and Philipa Veren, who owned this house, and when they moved to France we bought it and came to stay in Big Sur permanently. I became a full-time sculptor. I guess I have been ever since 1958, when I gave up teaching. I was carving vegetation then, like cactus and organic stuff inspired by Melissa's garden. Then my work changed from plants to people in trapped situation.

"In 1962, I had my first one-man show in San Francisco. I suppose people say 'one-woman show' now, but back then it didn't make a damn bit of difference to me. When I work I'm not a man or a woman.

Just a sculptor. I have a hell of a time with men in my sculptures though. Sometimes I do away with them altogether. For instance, there's one called 'Willy's mother.' I never meant to do her at all. I meant to do Willy, but then I heard about a woman who had forty cats and I thought, PERFECT. I'll have Willy's mother be totally involved with her cats."

She pointed over to a corner of the room. "You see I've carved twenty cats already, and I'm sick of it! But what was I saying? Oh, yes, men. Well, there was no father in the scene, so I thought I'd better put a little portrait of him, in wood of course, on the bookcase. He had no chin." She chuckled. "You see, I do have a nasty side. But really I'm not anti-male.

"My husband, and William Sawyer, whose gallery I show in, have supported me tremendously. And the men in Big Sur have supplied me with all sorts of wonderful wood for my carvings. Still, I'm very interested in how powerful women have become. I used to stir Bill's tea, put the sugar in, butter his bread and wait on the girls until they were teenagers. But when I became a full-time sculptor I had to ween everyone away from that.

"My family became my most realistic critics. Here again, I think it went back to my mother. We had to do a man's work to run that farm. She was the meekest little thing in the world until my father died, and then she became a very strong and powerful woman. So you see, we are what we are because of what we've been through. That's what I'm trying to show in my art work…with Willy's mother and her cats. She's the way she is because of what came before…because of what's happened in her life…like all of us."

There was a sudden loud gust of wind outside and then the sound of raindrops.

"Oh, my God!" shouted Barbara. "I'll have to get those legs in. Sorry I've talked so much. You must come back again so I can hear all about you and your life in Scotland."

After hearing about Bill and Barbara's life I could not imagine why anyone would want to hear about mine.

VIII
Keeking

It is a very strange thing to watch a partially paralyzed person having a temper tantrum, which was what Keeker was doing about 75 percent of the time. The left side of her face would be twisted up into a horrible grimace, and her left hand, knotted into a fist, would beat the air, while her left foot would stamp up and down like Rumpelstiltskin, but the right side of her body, facial expressions and all, would remain perfectly at peace.

The same was true of her happy moods, although they were a lot less frequent. When she walked, it was like a great dancing bear, shifting its weight from side to side, and although it took a tremendous amount of effort and concentration for her to be able to walk at all, there was something cheerful in the way she swayed.

When she would accomplish any of these physical challenges with success, the left side of her face would go crazy with smiles, and her left hand would wave an invisible banner of victory in the air. This was known as "Keeking," and when Keeker keeked, everyone was expected to keek along. People in her world were divided into two categories: those who could keek, and those who couldn't. Children, for instance were usually natural-born keekers. They didn't judge her weird behavior, but just laughed and imitated her dance, dancing right along with it. They screamed when they were angry, jumped up and down and giggled when they were glad, and wet their pants when they got too excited to remember they had to go. All of this was perfectly natural Keeker-type behavior. Politicians, businessmen, strict parents, and brain surgeons, of which we'd had to deal with quite a few, were NOT keekers.

But let me backtrack a bit here. There had not always been a Keeker. Once upon a time there had only been Sheilah, a wealthy debutante heiress, who was engaged to the heir of the Maytag washing machine company. I did not know her in that role because by the time I met her she had turned into a beatnik bar owner who wore black every day in mourning for the men who were dying in Vietnam.

It was when I was living in Scotland that I got word from my mother that Sheilah had suffered a stroke and was lying paralyzed in the hospital. I was working at the time as a stage manager for a play that the Royal Academy of Music and Drama in Glasgow was putting on, and so I cut an envelope-sized piece off of one of our red lighting gels and sent it to her. "Have one of the nurses hold this up to the light so that you can look at the world through rose-colored glasses," I wrote. It seemed silly, but it was all I could think of to say to someone in such a sad situation.

A year later she told me that it was the nicest thing anyone had done for her. Lying in her sterile white room with a shaved head and a steel plate in her skull, unable to move, the rose-colored glass had been one of the few joys she had.

By the time I came back from Scotland with my Scottish artist in tow, Sheilah was back home in the house next door to my mother's, attempting to live by herself, against all the advice of the doctors, who had told her that she would never walk again and could not possibly exist without the help of a nurse to feed and care for her.

Sheilah's sister, Suzannah, would often stop by to see if she needed help. Because she had apparently waddled like a duck when she was a baby, Suzannah was known as the Quacker. Sheilah, it seems, had always been afraid of spiders and bugs and would yell, "Keeeeek" if any of these creatures came near her, so now, although they were 28 and 35 years old, they still referred to each other as the Quacker and the Keeker.

When Robin and I arrived from Scotland, we had two suitcases and no money. My mother had no room for us, and we had no idea where we were going to go or how we would survive until Keeker, ever grateful for her rose-colored glasses, rescued us by saying we could live in the little room above her garage and help her take care of things. The room had a sofa bed, a wood stove, and a toilet in the form of a gallon-sized mayonnaise jar, but it was the best, and only, offer we'd had, and it was free.

This is when the Keeking began in earnest, and it was quite terrifying at first. Robin would be quietly painting some abstract thing, and I would be scanning the want ads in hopes of finding a job, when suddenly a long, loud shriek would pierce the silence.

"EEEEEEEEEEEEEEEE, Keeeeeeeeeeeeek. KEEEEEEEEEK." And I would go running down the stairs of the loft and into Sheilah's living room, wondering if she had fallen out of her wheel chair or off the porch, or what. But no, she was in the bathroom screaming. "Keeker wants, Keeker wants!"

"OK...it's all right...I'm here," I would pant breathlessly. "What does Keeker want?"

"EVERY FUCKING THING!" she'd yell. "I want to take a bath and the light is out and I can't get on a goddamn chair to change the bulb, and there's a spider in the bathtub, and if I lean over to get it out, I'll fall in and get stuck and EEEEEEEEEEEEEE, it makes me so crazy!"

"It's OK, Keeker, I'll help you," I'd say gently.

"NOOOO. I don't want anyone to help me. I want to be left alone."

"OK, I'm going right now. I'll go away and leave you alone."

"NOOO. I don't want you to leave. I want you to change the goddamn light bulb. I don't WANT you to help me, but I NEED you to help me, and I hate it!"

"I'm sorry," I'd say. "I'll just change the light bulb and run the bath and then I'll get out of here. I know it's hard. I'm sorry you're so upset."

"You *don't* know! You have no idea! And just stop being so fucking sorry all the time. I hate it when everybody's always so sorry for me."

And so began the delicate tight-rope walk of tending to Keeker. As her strength improved, so did her spirits, and her determination was absolutely astonishing. She began to walk with a walker, and when she was too tired to walk, she would crawl, and not just around the house but down a busy sidewalk in town, too. Several times she was stopped by the police who assumed she was either drunk or had escaped from a hospital.

By the time we went to live in the Big Sur house, Keeker was getting around pretty well, although she still could not drive on her own, so I had expected that when she was ready to move down to Partington she would call me to come and fetch her. I knew the time was getting closer because she had asked us to order firewood for the house, and she called frequently to find out what the weather was like. The cold made the steel plate in her head ache terribly.

It was a day in early spring when the ocean breeze was sending the sweet smell of jasmine and honeysuckle drifting in through our screen door when I heard a great commotion out in the driveway. A car horn was honking like crazy and old Booger was howling along in harmony. When I went out to investigate I found it was someone in a little VW Rabbit, and to my great amazement, out stepped Keeker.

She was doing her dance, kicking her one good leg in the air, and waving the old invisible flag. "Keek!" she yelled cheerfully. "Keek, Keek, my dears!"

We rushed down to greet her, and found that she was alone, and had driven the car here, all 200 miles, by herself.

"You won't believe it!" she said, dancing on first one foot and then the other. "I got a driver's license renewal in the mail. They didn't know I was paralyzed, and so I thought, well, what the hell! I had the Quacker take me out and help me buy an automatic car and here I am. I got so scared on the way down that I peed my pants twice! You see, my dears, it is just as I always suspected. God is a Keeker!"

Now that she could drive, Keeker's visits became more and more frequent, and as soon as the weather was warm enough, she moved to Partington for good. This proved to be a very difficult situation for all concerned because, although she wanted us to be near enough that we could hear her call, she wanted us to be neither visible, nor audible.

In all fairness to her, I knew that she suffered terribly from headaches and dizziness, and the large amounts of pot she smoked to alleviate the pain made her a little anxious and paranoid when people were around. But on our behalf, I must say that for us to sweep the pathways, water the plants and try to keep an active two-year-old from making any noise was a slightly impossible task.

My Libra nature wanted desperately for both sides to be happy, and so finally, we rigged up a sort of clothesline device which held a coffee can on a string with a bell attached to it. This was our source of communication, since Keeker's phone was permanently unplugged to prevent unwanted callers and conversations.

We were to remain quietly in our caretaker's quarters until we heard the jingle-bell can making its way up the line to our house. I would then tiptoe out onto the porch to discover what sort of message awaited us. Sometimes it would be something reasonable, like, "I want to sit out on the patio and read and I don't want to see anyone, so please don't do yardwork today." Or, "I'm going to drive into town, so today would be a good day for you to do the watering."

Other times it would be a stern lecture, such as, "Haven't I told you to pee on the avocado tree? It doesn't look very good and I'm sure it needs more pee. If you don't want to climb up there, save it in jars and pour it on once a week."

The tree stood on a precarious ledge above her house and it took a steep climb up a rock wall to get to it. Once there, you had to position yourself just right, pants down, or you'd roll off down the hill.

I thought this request utterly ridiculous. Whatever nutrient urine contained, I had seen hundreds of perfectly healthy groves of avocado trees in my day and nobody was peeing on them. One would have

DRINKING TO KINDNESS

had to hire an army of beer-drinking farm workers to get the job done. And how was I supposed to encourage proper toilet training in a child who saw his mother hanging over a cliff aiming a stream at a tree trunk?. Totally ridiculous.

The clothesline messages were sometimes hurtful, sometimes gloomy, sometimes outrageously funny, but always eccentric. Once, late at night, I heard the bell going and fearful that she might be sick, or need help, I rushed outside to find a note which said, "Did you ever do it in the backseat of a Ford at a drive-in movie?" And then there was the coffin. Having come so close to death, Keeker had given a lot of thought to how she wanted to be buried, and one day, while sipping a glass of plum wine on the veranda, she had hit upon the perfect plan, a plan so exciting that it made her jump up and start keeking for joy.

She would design and build her very own coffin, and have all of her friends paint pictures or write poems inside so that she could enjoy them in the afterlife. Meanwhile, she planned to put her sleeping bag inside it and nap there from time to time to get comfortable with the idea.

We heard about this plan in the usual way when the coffee can came jingling up with its daily message. The note read, "Kent, the carpenter, is coming over today to take measurements for my coffin. Do you think cedar or pine? Cedar would keep the bugs out. And while he's here I am going to ask him if he can get this bidet out of my bathroom. Who needs an asswasher anyway?"

"What does it all mean?" asked Robin, shaking his head.

"I don't know," I said, "but I think Kent, the carpenter, better fit me for a coffin, too, while he's at it, because I'm not sure how much more of this I can handle."

It was not too long after this that Gary and Vicki bought the old Bradford property down on lower Partington. They didn't want to live in the cramped little apartment above the candle shop forever, and the Bradford place was in such bad shape that it was going cheap, by Big Sur standards.

There was a main house, with a little one-room apartment below it, a huge building that looked like an airplane hanger, which had served as a lithographic studio, and several small illegal dwellings, such as a tree house and a small cabin made of scrap wood that sat in the bushes on the edge of the cliff. The place was a goldmine of rentable possibilities, as folks in Big Sur would pay up to $600 a month to live in a goat shed, or, like the Nashs', under a tarp that might someday become a greenhouse.

Knowing the situation we were in, Gary offered to rent us the airplane hanger and we went down to look at it. It had no doors or windows, just a wall that slid to one side to let the huge lithographs in and out, but it did have a bathroom. There were several large holes in the roof and the place was ankle deep in water. It was so hopelessly in need of repair, that I couldn't see how we could ever live there, but we were by no means the only people in Big Sur looking for a shelter, and Gary said if we didn't want it, there were a lot of others waiting in line. Then, by some miracle, my Uncle Paige from Mendocino stopped by for a visit, and things took on a whole new light.

IX
Binker

Binker – what I call him – is a secret of my own
And Binker is the reason why I never feel alone.
Playing in the nursery, sitting on the stair,
Whatever I am busy at, Binker will be there.
Oh, Daddy is clever, he's a clever sort of man,
And Mummy is the best since the world began,
And Nanny is Nanny, and I call her Nan,
But they're not
Like
Binker.
             —A. A. Milne

Uncle Paige Binker was tall and thin and partially bald. He had a stubby beard, twinkly eyes and a pipe sticking out of the corner of his mouth. He looked like a combination of Popeye the sailor man and Don Quixote, and indeed, he must have fancied himself as the knight errant, for the name "Rocinante" was painted in faded letters on the side of his old gray pickup.

Paige had been a school friend of my father's and had ended up marrying my father's sister, Peg. Later, he went to work as a produce man in a Safeway store. When I was young and I went to visit the Binker family, I got to experience all sorts of interesting things from the world of produce. They were the first people to ever serve me a mysterious and delicious fruit called a cantaloupe, which I had never even heard of. When I questioned my mother about it, she said that the smell of cantaloupes made her vomit and she simply could not stand to have them in the house.

Aunt Peg and Uncle Paige were later divorced and my uncle took early retirement, moving off to Mendocino County to build himself a little cabin in the wilderness on some property that belonged to a friend. Art had always been his hobby, and now he could pursue it in earnest. I loved to watch him sketch because he was left-handed and it always seemed funny to me that someone could work, as Paige did, with the paper turned sideways at such a funny angle. His drawings were very sensitive and lyrical for such a gangly sort of of fellow.

Paige built his home like a nomadic pioneer. It was twenty feet square with every nook and cranny carefully planned out; kitchen space, storage area, and sleeping bunk. It was not nailed, but bolted together, so that if he decided to pull up stakes and move elsewhere, he could dismantle it, pack it in the back of Rocinante and gallop.

Although he lived a rather solitary life up in the piney woods, he was a man who appreciated the finer things in life. He was a gourmet cook, savored a fine wine, read good books, attended local theater, and enjoyed a gin martini with a green olive every night at five o'clock.

Therefore, we were delighted one day when out of the blue Paige and Rocinante pulled up into our driveway, having come to call.

Robin and Paige had been soul mates since they'd first met when we'd come back from Scotland. Robin, the misunderstood artist, stifled by this foreign land of commercialism, and Paige, the Sage, wise old man of the mountains, who had foregone art for a life among fruits and vegetables in order to support his family. They sat for hours, puffing on pipes, spouting poetry and philosophy, and toasting one another's brilliance.

Later they would usually stroll down to Harrydick's place in the moonlight to philosophize some more. Here was a member of the brotherhood even older and wiser than Paige. Harrydick would curse them, advise them, and dismiss them in the wee hours with a farewell song of triumph.

I was usually the odd one out in these male bonding sessions, but I knew that fate had sent Paige here at just the right time for a reason, and after one very late night of drinking, I suggested we take an early morning walk to breathe in a little fresh oxygen and blow the cobwebs out. I wanted Paige to see the Bradford place and tell us whether or not the devastated studio was salvageable or not. If anyone could visualize redemption, Paige could.

For me, carrying my son in a backpack and wishing only for a warm and safe environment for my family, the airplane hanger was a dark and dismal swamp, smelling of mildew and despair. For Robin it, was a mind-boggling project, far too technical and time consuming to deal with when one had art to do.

Paige lit his pipe and gazed around the room. He tiptoed through the puddled floor in his brown suede birkenstocks, tapping walls and feeling for studs like an orthopedic surgeon searching for broken bones. He peeked in cupboards and closets, examined a small room with a toilet and sink and found they were plugged and not working. He checked out a large sunken cement tub which had apparently been used for bathing lithographs, and rolled back a huge sliding door in the back of the room to reveal a majestic view of Partington Canyon and the hills beyond. To Paige the hanger was a faded masterpiece waiting to be restored.

He turned to us, eyes twinkling, pipe puffing, a secretive grin on his face. He always had a funny way of shuffling his feet and moving his head from side to side when he was pleased, like a shy child who has just been given a compliment and doesn't know what to say.

"Well?" I asked anxiously. "Is it salvageable?"

"Ha ha ha," he laughed, smiling and puffing. "Ha ha ha."

"PAIGE, tell me! Is this a mess or what? Stop laughing."

"Look at that view, kid," he said, ignoring me. "Pow!" He hit himself square in the middle of his forehead with the palm of his hand. "Look at the damn view!"

"Aye," Robin said strolling out onto the deck cautiously. He didn't want to seem too enthusiastic about a project that might involve him. "Aye, it's a lovely sight, but we've got no money and Gary has offered it to us pretty much as is."

"Scrounge, kid," said Paige. "We can always use scrounge. There's a lot of it around on the Mendocino property, and there is bound to be stuff around here, too."

"Scrounge?" Robin looked puzzled.

"Old scrap wood, old doors, bits and pieces, a window or two. We can make that sunken vat thing into a bathtub...see if Gary can get us a nice redwood slab from the woodyard in the back of the gallery; that would make a nice kitchen counter, and then some Dutch doors here, out to the porch, and a little white paint...it will all come together, kid. I'll leave tomorrow and be back in a week or so."

My spirits soared. We were now going to be permanent residents of Big Sur...not visitors, not caretakers, but renters, with a place of our own. The land and the locals were no longer strange to me. I had accepted their ways and become one with the weird. I had a job, a car, and soon I would have a house bigger than any structure I, or anyone else I knew, had ever lived in!

The "week or so" went by and then some. We waited eagerly for the scrounge to appear. We knew that Rocinante had not been well, and perhaps the trip to and from Big Sur had injured the old beast beyond repair. Paige had no phone in his little cabin, so there was nothing to do but wait, and hope, and listen as the bell on the clothesline can made its way up and down between the houses.

Keeker had taken the news of our move quite cheerfully. I think the tension of having us so nearby when she wanted to be alone was getting to her, too, and she now planned to use the caretaker's quarters as a guest house for Susannah and the folks from the Zen Center that she had befriended. Now that everything had been peacefully resolved we were all eager to get on with it.

Ever since I had connected with the earth spirit it had become my pattern to get up early, before Jamie and Robin, and go sit on the outermost cliff point and watch the dawn. One such morning it had been a little over a month since Paige had gone and I was feeling restless and depressed, so I decided instead of sitting on the point I would walk down the hill to the Bradford place and take another look at the studio.

It took about twenty minutes and the ridge was all pink and lavender in the early morning light as I rounded the last corner of the driveway. Even before I saw the campfire I could smell coffee brewing. Sure enough there was old Rocinante parked at the foot of the hill and Uncle Paige squatting alongside the fire, puffing on his pipe. I went running up to hug him, laughing with relief.

"Hi, kid," he twinkled. "Wasn't sure we'd make it. The old truck's so loaded down we had a hell of a time...just rolled in last night so I thought I'd make camp here. Tell Rrrrrobin to get his Scottish arse down here so we can start unloading."

X
Easy Street

It was rumored that to get Alan Eichman to show up for a job all you had to do was think of him; send him a sort of telepathic phone call, and he'd be there, because, of course, he did not have a telephone in his tent. Most of the time this system worked and he would come peddling slowly down the highway on his bike, saying he had gotten the message and asking what it was that we needed done. Other times we'd wait an hour or so and Gary would get nervous and pace the floor, complaining that pine needles needed to be raked, and the spiky purple echium plants were threatening to take over the parking lot unless they were pruned back.

At times like these I happily volunteered to go off to Partington Canyon and hike up the hill in search of Alan. To me it would be a welcome break in the day, a paid adventure.

The mouth of the canyon was accessible only by way of a narrow path covered in brush. Not many people bothered to explore it, but since working at the gallery, I had gotten to know Alan and had given him a lift home several times.

The first time he had invited me to come up and see his home and have a cup of tea. I had followed him, hiking half a mile up a steep dark redwood trail until we came to a tent under the redwoods. It was just big enough for the two of us to sit comfortably and drink tea brewed on his campfire.

Often, when I'd hike up to alert him to the needs of the gallery's garden, I'd reprimand him for not answering his telepathic phone. He'd say, "I heard you, but I'm really enjoying this book I'm reading today and I don't feel like working."

The outside world really didn't matter to him one way or another. They could take him or leave him. I wished I, too, could be so nonchalant about making a living.

Alan was delighted when he found that we were going to be his neighbors, living in the Bradford studio, a mere 600 feet up a sheer cliff above his mysterious gnome house, which sat buried down in the redwoods. He asked if it might be possible to catch a ride into town and do some laundry on my next town day.

I told him I would be going in on Friday morning around nine o'clock. I wondered if he even had a clock. He struck me as the sort of creature who got up when it was light, ate when hungry and went to sleep when it got dark...none of this daylight-savings stuff.

On Friday, I rushed around getting Jamie dressed and fed, sorted washing, made grocery lists for food, building materials and art supplies. When I dashed out of the door I found Alan standing beside the VW with a huge backpack at his feet.

"You didn't need to hike up with all that," I said looking in amazement at his heavy load of laundry. "I was planning to pick you up down on the highway."

"It's OK," he smiled. "I have my own road."

I looked puzzled. There was only one road up and down the ridge that I knew of. He smiled again and nodded toward the cliff face. "I came up by rope," he said.

I was horrified looking over at the steep drop. The tops of giant redwood trees were just starting to appear out of the mist below.

"Well, it's not a rope all the way. Part of the way there's a ladder. Then you hoist yourself up by some long weeds and jump over a ravine. Then you hoist yourself up by another rope through the buffalo grass. After that there's a climb through an old culvert and pretty soon you're up here. I call it Easy Street."

"I call it insanity," I said.

I piled Alan and Jamie and the laundry into the VW bug and waved goodbye to Robin and Paige as we headed for town. I no longer left Jamie home, since the men were so busy working that they couldn't watch him.

Alan pointed out all sorts of places as we drove along. He knew were there were inaccessible beaches, abandoned homesteads with fruit trees that still bore fruit, limestone caves, and the remains of old shipwrecks.

"Have you been here all your life?" I asked.

"No, only about eight years. I rode my bike here from San Francisco one day, and I've been here ever since."

We were halfway to town when Alan asked if I'd mind stopping for driftwood. The only thing I could imagine him wanting it for was to make a campfire to cook on, and I tried to imagine the three of us, the laundry, the groceries and a load of firewood piled in the back seat of the VW. But after all, he was sort of a guest and I didn't want to be impolite so I agreed.

I strapped Jamie up in the backpack and followed Alan down a narrow path bordered by ice plant of all colors, down to a little cove where sea lions barked and the waves were gentle and green. There was no driftwood anywhere in sight, but Alan seemed to have forgotten that this was why we'd come. He was investigating everything. He picked things up, sniffed them, turned them over and over and muttered to himself. There was an old skeleton of a car, half-filled with sand and seaweed, and the way he inspected it I almost expected him to get in and take it for a test drive, but then something else caught his eye. An old blue bucket. He gave it the examination, turning it over and then filling it with water to see if it leaked. It didn't, and he started back up the path toward the car, bucket in hand, looking quite pleased.

"What about the driftwood?" I asked.

"Oh, I've got that right here," he said, pulling a small wooden plank out of his back pocket. "I just wanted to carve myself a spoon."

At the laundromat Alan walked right up to the big heavy-duty machine that I thought people only used for washing rugs. I gathered he had some serious washing to do. I busied myself with my own laundry and then we went off to shop while the clothes were getting cleaned.

I had bits and pieces of hardware to buy for Paige and two tubes of watercolors to get for Robin. Alan had said he was going to the paperback book exchange and would meet me back at the laundromat in an hour.

When I got back he was there, as promised, folding thing. He folded and folded and folded and folded…jeans in various stages of decay, worn out shirts and shredded towels and endless socks, none of which seemed to match. Alan explained that he used socks, not just for footwear, but also for handkerchiefs, potholders and dish cloths.

He pulled up his pant leg to show me that even as we spoke he was wearing four pairs of socks on each foot. This was because once when he was riding his bike it had gotten a flat tire, and being miles from a gas station where he could pump it up, he had filled the flat with socks and ridden successfully back home. You just could not have too many socks.

"I know where we can find some pieces of glass," Alan said cheerfully when the washing was done.

Pieces of glass…pieces of glass? Had I mentioned wanting glass? It wasn't on my town list, but then perhaps, like the driftwood, it was on his. "OK, lead on," I said.

We went to a beach over by Fisherman's Wharf where there were pelicans and sea otters, but no pieces of glass. We watched fishing boats come into the harbor while Jamie toddled after seagulls.

"This has been really wonderful," I said, "but I have to get home and start dinner. It will be getting dark soon."

"I brought a flashlight," said Alan.

Of course, I thought. Who else would think to bring a flashlight on a grocery shopping trip, but then he *was* prepared for all occasions.

When we got back to Big Sur we stopped at the top of the ridge to watch the sky turning all pink and purple in the sunset. Jamie was teetering along the cliff top, waving his hand and saying, "Bye, Bye town…Bye, bye sun." It had certainly been a very different and interesting kind of town day for me and I turned to thank Alan and tell him how much I'd enjoyed it, but he was gone, along with the sun, sliding his way back down Easy Street.

XI
The Future King of Scots

The studio progressed in leaps and bounds of patchwork glory as truckloads of broken and abandoned building supplies were sanded, rehinged, reglazed and repainted. The paint covered a multitude of sins, creating a very dramatic and startling transformation as the two artists went at it.

My only input was the floor. I had grown up near a family who lived in a Frank Lloyd Wright house with red-tiled floors, and now I insisted that once the cement slab floor of the studio was drained and scrubbed, it must be painted brick red.

The walls, of course, were white, for displaying paintings. The woodwork, kitchen cupboards, bookshelves, closet doors, window frames, etc., were done in a bright royal blue enamel to hide the fact that they were pieced together with all sorts of scraps. Someone had donated a huge yellow carpet and some lime green chairs.

Since the house was basically all one gigantic room, it was beginning to take on a kind of Big Top circus tent effect with Uncle Paige Binker, wearing nothing but an old pair of shorts, a carpenter's belt, and his birkenstock sandals, the proud ring master in the center of it all.

My relatives worried about Jamie growing up in this environment of eccentric adults with no other children to play with, but as I had tried to explain to them, Jamie had never really been a child. He had been nearly ten pounds at birth and looked, as one of our friends had commented, "Like a wise little Buddha in a baby suit."

He was a fussy baby for the first year, seemingly frustrated and annoyed because he wanted to walk and talk and do things that his infant's body was not ready to do. He nursed, reluctantly. I thought that breast milk was not only better, it was free, but just as soon as possible he began to reject milk, formula, and my lovingly cooked and strained vegetables and demand meat.

When, at last, he started to talk, he began to babble endlessly about a lighthouse. It seemed almost to be his motivation for learning to speak. It appeared to be a very depressing subject as he would often break down in tears when telling us about it. I scanned the coast on our town trips for any signs of a lighthouse, but there was only Point Sur, which was almost always hidden in fog, and it didn't seem to interest him much.

I looked through his baby books for pictures, and questioned Harrydick, who had become like a surrogate grandfather, but none of us remembered talking about lighthouses. There was one place, near Carmel Highlands, where Jamie would get very excited. Some construction company was putting up a series of white Spanish-style houses with red tile roofs along the beach front. When we got to this section of the coast, he would press his nose to the window and shout, "There they are! There are my houses!"

I always questioned him about it, explaining that those were not *our* houses and we didn't know the people that lived there. "Why do you like them?" I'd ask. "We've never lived in a house like that before."

"Not NOW!" Jamie would say in exasperation. "When I was a big person...BEFORE, when I was BIG. My town looked like that and I lived at the lighthouse and my cats slept up beside the light because it was warm, and I had a nice garden, but then the bad men came." Here he would start to cry. "They tore up my garden and they wrecked my house...and they hurt me, and they hurt my lady. I HATE the bad men. Don't let them come back, Mommy. Don't let the bad men come back and hurt us."

I questioned doctors, but they all insisted that he must have seen a scary television show or a movie, but we didn't have a TV and we never went to movies because we couldn't afford it.

At last I came across an article in a women's magazine, written by a child psychologist who was researching past life trauma. Everything the author said coincided perfectly with Jamie's strange behavior. Delighted that I had found someone who could solve the mystery, I wrote the psychologist a letter and received a very nice response which said that he was overwhelmed with case studies of children who recalled their past lives and could not help us personally at the moment, but he did encourage me to listen patiently while Jamie talked and not to tell him that he was being silly and just imagining things.

As soon as we were somewhat established in the studio I decided to try my hand once more at putting in a vegetable garden. I felt it would be a practical addition to our minuscule budget and therapeutic for Jamie, who seemed to have been so fond of the garden that the "bad men" had ruined.

Robin refused to believe that any son of his could possibly have a problem, psychological or otherwise, and had maintained since the day of his birth that Jamie was the chosen one who would someday go back to Scotland and reclaim the throne.

"So, how's the future King of Scots this morning?" Robin would say.

And as time went on, Jamie began to worry less and less about the lighthouse incident and accept his inevitable new assignment as an up-and-coming heir.

I had an old red velvet blouse that had gotten too small for me, and Jamie soon took to wearing it, belted at the waist, along with a golden cardboard crown we had acquired from some fast-food restaurant on one of our town trips. Dressed in his royal attire and little hiking boots, he would take his toy rake and shovel and go off to spend happy hours working in the garden.

One day when Paige had gone off to Monterey to fetch some locks and latches to put the final touches on doors and windows, I was washing dishes in the kitchen when I heard Robin and Jamie shouting up to the house from the garden below. I supposed they had left a trowel or a packet of seeds behind and wanted me to bring them down, so I went out onto the deck and looked over the edge where I could view the garden.

We had fenced it in to keep out the deer, but the fence was a pretty flimsy, chicken-wire affair. Anything that really wanted to get in probably could have without much trouble. That's why it was so startling to see what the commotion was all about. It struck me that it looked very like a scene from Antoine de Saint Exupery's *Little Prince*, for there, perched on the potting shed roof, sat Robin, in his dirty overalls, and Jamie in his red velvet robe and crown. Below them, surrounding the garden fence, snorting and pawing at the ground, was a herd of not-too-friendly looking wild boar.

"What shall we do?" Robin shouted. "I don't like the look of these bloody bastards."

"I don't know what the hell to do!" I said. "Throw things at them. Turn the hose on them."

"But that might make them mad and then they'd charge us and knock down the fence. I've got to get Jamie out of here."

"Look at all the piggies, Mama!" Jamie called up to me. "Daddy says they're hungry."

The boars were now making themselves comfortable all around the garden. Several had decided to settle down for a nap. They showed no signs whatsoever of leaving.

"Don't panic," I shouted. "I'll think of something." But I couldn't. I tried to remember what the locals had told me about wild boar in the past, but the only thing I could recall was that they were usually mean, didn't like to be messed around with, and the only good boar was a barbecued one.

I finally took off running down the road to where Larry and Louise were living and Larry came to my rescue. He loved a good adventure. "This is outrageous! This is so funny!" he kept saying. "We should call Walter Trotter. He'd come over with a gun and shoot them all, or else he'd just pick them up in his teeth and shake them to death."

Somehow, with Larry and I yelling and shooing, throwing rocks and squirting the garden hose, we finally convinced the pigs to reluctantly ramble off back down the hill into the chaparral while Jamie and Robin dashed out of the garden and up the hill to our house.

Paige was a little hesitant to sleep outside at his camp site for the next few evenings, and I felt uneasy about the rambles around the property that Jamie often took, but he wasn't at all afraid of the wild piggies and actually seemed to be sort of fond of them.

He liked to walk down the road and visit Louise. She made up a song for him which he would sing to himself as he trotted home in his little robe and crown, with all the valiant confidence that one would hope for in a future king.

> "Boars in the bushes
> Shoo boars, shoo
> Boars in the flower beds
> Can't get you
> Boars in the vegetables
> Snortin', too
> Skip all the way home my darlin'."

XII
Poets and Painters

Louise claimed that the spirits of the Bradford house had spoken to her and said that a city family with two children would soon rent the main house, but as things turned out it was the Parson brothers who finally moved in to the top part. Deborah Medow, a massage and yoga teacher from Esalen Institute, took up residence in the tiny apartment under the deck, on the hillside just below our big studio house.

Warriors, rebels, artists and poets, the Parson boys were always drinking and fighting, crying and singing, loving and losing, and when they couldn't find anyone else to beat up they would beat up each other. Stephen, the oldest, had come to Big Sur from Los Angeles to recover from a broken heart and a back injury and to bury himself in his jewelry-making business. Kevin arrived some weeks later. He, too, seemed to be suffering from some sort of melancholy disorder. He was the poet. His verses flowed as long and deep as the steady turbulent river of brandy, wine and beer that ran through their living room.

Kevin could compose three pages of verse, and then put down the paper and recite the entire creation to you by memory, word for emotional word, head cocked, voice trembling, and eyes locked on yours with heartfelt sincerity...on...and on...and on.

With the completion of the reconstruction project, Paige had gone back off to Mendocino to the peace and sanity of his cabin in the pines. I hoped things in our lives might settle down for awhile, but when Robin met Kevin it was as though the two long lost sages of Atlantis had resurfaced, reunited in the new world at last.

They flung poems at each other like sentimental hand grenades. They whimpered and wept with the joy of their creations, danced and screamed in mutual admiration at the image that a single, eloquent adjective might produce. Once they found that they had both written a poem abut a bum on a park bench covered in newspapers. The laughing and crying and drinking of toasts went on and on, until for some reason they had an ice-cream fight, tossing butter brickle all over themselves, our newly painted walls, and the lime green chairs.

When I begged for them to stop, they defended themselves, grandly. "But we are POETS," they cried, "and we wear our ice cream like war bonnets, like Pulitzer medals of honor, like corsages pinned to the bosoms of our dreams."

Egotistical pathos puke! I thought to myself, as I mopped up the walls and furniture. *How do I always end up getting involved with people like this?*

As the chaos continued, there was a timid tapping at the front door and Deborah the Yogi crept in looking as thin and frail as Ghandi after a three-month fast. She seem to live almost exclusively on a diet of brown rice, sprouts and wheat grass juice...spiritually purifying vegetarian sustenance without much joy, fat or flavor to it.

She peered suspiciously at the poets, and then, carefully skirting them, she made her way over to my corner of the room. Her arms were full of all sorts of strange things; animal skins, bones and feathers and beads. "May I put these down here?" she asked me. "I need you to help me become a Zulu."

"A Zulu?" I asked.

"I'm going to a costume party, and I want to be a Zulu, but I'm not sure how."

Robin dashed off to his art department and came back with a tray full of paints. He and Kevin each took a leg, and I took her head. We painted her black with red, yellow and white stripes. Then we draped her body with skins and beads and bones. She was a wonderfully impressive sight, but the paint was hardening like plaster, and by the time we were finished painting, she could barely move. "I was hoping to be able to dance," she said sadly. "There's going to be a good band."

"Just sort of stand in one place and stamp your feet and chant. Booga Loooo, Boooga Loooo, Hubba Bubba, Booga Looo." Robin demonstrated his impression of primitive dance. "Isn't that what Zulus do?"

"Beats the hell out of me," said Kevin, for once, relatively speechless.

Later that night Stephen came home, fresh from the bar and smelling of beer, blood and aftershave. He put on some rock and roll, lit a stick of incense, and tried to pick a fight with his brother.

Later still, Deborah came back from the dance, her paint cracking and her bones and feathers drooping. Stephen made an unsuccessful effort to seduce her. Jamie and I curled up on the big red corduroy pillow next to the fireplace and drifted off to sleep to the endless droning of poetry.

As time went on, what I began to refer to as the "poetic injustice" continued, and my patience grew thin. I had managed to get Jamie into The Gazebo at Esalen, which was sort of a new, experimental concept in pre-school at the time, where the children planted gardens, meditated, and were sort of free to interact and solve problems among themselves without a lot of adult intervention.

We couldn't really afford it, but for Jamie's sake, I felt he needed to be around more children and Robin claimed that he needed more time to paint. However, there were many times when I'd come home from the gallery tired and talked out from dealing with tourists all day, to find the Partington philosophers locked in drunken discussion and oblivious to my none too subtle hints that the party was over.

It got so sometimes I wouldn't even bother going home after work if I didn't feel up to dealing with it. I would head up, instead, to Harrydick's place where I knew I could depend on a kiss and a hug, a good strong drink and some sound advice with no bullshit involved.

"I'm sorry to bother you, Ross," I'd say.

"Honey, I LOVE it when you bother me!"

"I just need a little peaceful chat."

"I LOVE to chat with you. Let's have a drink."

"Well, maybe just a glass of wine, if you have it."

"Oh, to hell with wine. Let's have a *real* drink."

"Thank God for Harrydick Ross," I'd say, and curl up in front of the wood stove and start to relax.

"Is it that artist of yours again?" he'd ask.

"Um hum."

"What the hell is that guy up to now?"

"Well, Jamie's in school now, and he needs new clothes, shoes and things. I'm working a lot and we're trying to pay rent and Robin's art doesn't sell very fast...I mean if he'd only do more commercial stuff it might sell better...but then I get home and there are all sorts of people hanging around talking and getting drunk. They stay late and I can't go to bed because the bed is in the middle of the living room, so there's nowhere to go to be alone and...I don't know. I just get depressed."

"When I was Robin's age I took my portfolio under my arm and walked the streets of San Francisco asking every gallery and printer and newspaper and magazine if they could use my work. I pushed myself. I *had* to. Now why the hell doesn't he go out and do that?"

"I don't know. I'd have to drive him to the city...and take him all over the place looking for galleries. He's too shy to go into galleries and talk to people, so I'd end up having to do it for him...and I've got to stay here and work."

"Oh, balls," said Harrydick. "He needs to be more aggressive."

And so we would go on until I either felt more cheerful or started getting a guilt complex about the fact that I was neither spending quality time with my son nor taking care of dinner for my family.

Other days, when I was not in the mood for Harrydick's stern lectures and sound advice, I would go down into the canyon for a more ethereal type of visit with Alan. I had finally braved Easy Street one day in a fit of rage and disgust, when I could no longer tolerate the ranting and raving of artists and poets. It was, as Alan had described it, a long slide down a steep culvert on your rear, a mighty leap over a ravine, a hair-raising climb down a rickety ladder, and then a terrifying slide down a rope into the bottle green world under the redwood canopy.

Weak-kneed and panting I had finally found my way to Alan's little tent, where he graciously wiped out an old cracked cup with one of his many socks and poured me a cup of tea.

Something was bubbling away on the top of the camp fire, so I asked what was cooking.

"Barley," he replied. "I've been reading about Egypt. Did you know they have found barley husks in the intestines of ancient Egyptian mummies? Some part of me is really into Egypt. I've decided to build myself a pyramid up on the hill. I'm too close to the creek down here. All I ever hear is water rushing by, day and night. Sometimes the sound fills my whole head and I can't even turn on the water tap because I don't want to let any more of that creek into my world. A nice pyramid up on the hill would be so much more peaceful. I could just sit there and read and eat barley. More tea?"

"Poets and painters and gnomes building pyramids," I muttered to myself as I struggled back up the ravine, clutching at roots and poison oak vines. "Where the hell does a person go for a little sanity around here? I can just see my tombstone now: 'She died trying to make it up Easy Street.'"

XIII
Chewey

It was never easy trying to coax my mother, who had been born in the plains country of Kansas, to come and visit me in Big Sur. She now lived in the Bay Area near Stanford University so the trip to Big Sur meant a two-hour drive on the busy 101 freeway and another hour on the twisty cliff tops of Highway One, which absolutely terrified her.

Our car was lucky if it made it to and from Monterey without incident, and we could not risk pushing it to go and see her, so our visits were primarily by phone. On the rare occasions when I could coerce her to come and stay with us, the visits would be brief and tense because she claimed that seeing the ocean gave her the creeps. "Those big horrible waves are always *reaching* for you. And it's so WET!" she'd say.

It wasn't that she was afraid of water, for I had often heard stories of how she used to swim in a pond full of water moccasins when she lived in Texas. It was difficult to understand now she could find a wave more terrifying than a deadly snake, but she had definite opinions on these things.

The snakes were considered "cute" swimming along with their little heads above water. Waves were big and wet and they wanted to grab you and pull you out to sea, and besides they smelled of fish. "Ugh!"

Another one of her phobias was Indians. I never did understand this because she loved the red rock country of the Southwest and always came home with a Navajo rug, but perhaps she had seen one too many bad westerns. She felt that Indians, like waves, were also, "out to get you." That's why it was unfortunate that, when at long last I had managed to lure her down for a visit, we were invaded by Chewey.

It was all Alan's fault. He sometimes picked the most inconvenient times to drop in, but then I guess I did it to him, too, so it was hard to be annoyed. Still, Alan was a bit different from most folks and I had hoped that the usual crowd of lotus eaters would keep their distance for the weekend and let us have a good family gossip.

The sun had set and the threatening waves were now hidden from sight by darkness. We were just beginning to relax, sip a little sweet vermouth and catch up on each other's news, when Alan poked his head in the door. He didn't wait for an invitation, but came strolling in and helped himself to a drink, delighted to see that we had company…and a new brain to pick.

I introduced Alan to my mother and she shook hands reluctantly, since he was a little grubby after his climb up Easy Street.

"What do you think of Egypt?" Alan asked my mother. "I'm thinking maybe I used to hang out there in one of my lives."

"Egypt?" she said, looking perplexed. "I don't know. I very seldom think about Egypt."

We chatted a bit more and Alan told her about the barley in the mummies' stomachs. For some reason he kept looking expectantly at the front door, and I hoped that this might be a sign that he felt he was intruding and was planning to go soon, but after a few minutes, he said, "I wonder what happened to Chewey?"

"Chewey?" I said.

"He was just going to tie up the mule and be right in."

"Mule?" said my mother.

I went over to the door and peered out into the darkness.

"Knockus, knockus," said a voice an inch away from my ear.

I jumped about a foot, then I opened the door a little wider to shed some light on the speaker and screamed. At first I thought he was naked, but after my eyes began to focus in the dark, I could see that he had a sort of loin cloth draped around his waist. He was short and stocky, with long, black, tangled hair held back from his face by a red bandana head band. His deep-brown, deer-like eyes stared in at me. My heart sank. There was no doubt about it. Chewey was definitely an Indian of the most primitive variety.

"Knockus, knockus," he said again, tapping his fist against the wall in case I had not understood the first time.

"Oh, God. I suppose you'll have to come in," I said, standing aside to let him pass.

"This is Chewey." Alan beamed happily. "He's an Indian."

"Oh, Jesus!" cried my mother.

Jamie, who had curled up beside his grandmother, put on his crown because this was obviously the kind of special occasion where a king may be called upon to take control.

Chewey made a bee line for the kitchen stove where I had a pot of vegetable soup and a tray of biscuits ready for dinner. He peeked into the soup pot and sniffed. "Chewey needs meat," he said.

"That's vegetable soup. There isn't any meat in it, and please don't eat the biscuits!" I snapped.

"There's wine, Chewey," Alan said, holding up the bottle of Cinzano.

"Chewey wants happy tabac," said the Indian.

"What's happy tabac?" asked Robin.

"Marajuana," said Alan. "Chewey likes to get stoned."

"No. We don't have any of that," I said.

Chewey looked disappointed. "OK. Chewey drink wine," he said, grabbing the bottle and tipping it up to his mouth.

"He doesn't bother with cups," Alan explained, unnecessarily.

Suddenly Chewey caught sight of my mother who had wedged herself into a corner beside the fireplace, hoping to escape any raping or scalping that might be about to take place. He stared at her for a moment and then slapped his naked thigh with delight.

"Hey, old woman!" he cried. "Chewey will sing for you!"

"No. No...tell him no, please," she pleaded.

But Chewey had already spotted my guitar and attacked the instrument like a hungry wolf attacking a bone. He pulled at it and beat on it, throwing his head back to howl and moan, at the same time hopping around the room on first one bare foot and then the other.

"Isn't Chewey cool?" Alan grinned.

Jamie went for his little water pistol. With a crown and a water gun he could feel relatively safe.

When the song, if you could call it that, was over, there came from outside an even more awesome howl. I feared that perhaps the rest of his tribe were on their way, or perhaps his song had lured a yeti out of the Ventana wilderness.

"It's his mule," Alan explained. "She's pregnant and can't be moved for awhile, so I told Chewey he could probably hang out here for a few days.

That did it. Twisty roads, threatening waves and dark, sheer cliffs...none of them were as as terrifying as spending the weekend with Cro-Magnon and his pregnant mule. My mother was out the door and gone in a flash, and it was a very long time before we could talk her into coming to visit again.

XIV
Laurel and Hardy Contruction

On one of our many scrounge-collecting trips, we had acquired an old washing machine. It sat for months in the storage area just outside the front door. My diaper-washing days were long over, thank God, but now with Jamie going to school and me working full time instead of just part, we had more laundry than my once-a-week town trip could handle, so I asked around to see if anyone knew how to hook up the plumbing for our washer.

Everyone told me to ask a Trotter, so when I accidentally overhead someone say, "Hey, Trotter!" in the local deli one day, I decided to be bold and go ask this guy if I could get him to help me out.

It was not Walter, but sort of a younger version of the same, big and burly and tough looking with his brown curly hair pulled back in a pony tail.

"Excuse me," I began, "do you do any plumbing?"

"Somebody just killed my favorite fucking dog!" he replied, glowering at me.

"Oh, dear. I'm really sorry," I said, wondering how I could work washing machine hook-ups into this conversation that had evidently gotten off on the wrong foot.

"You think *you're* sorry! I'm gonna kill the son of a bitch who did it."

"Here's your coffee, Richard," said the girl behind the counter. "Your sandwich will be up in a minute."

"Maybe I could just call you some other time," I said, thinking I had better just slip away.

"Nah. It's OK. I need the money. What's your problem?"

"I just need someone to hook up a washing machine for me. I live up at the old Bradford place on Partington. In the studio."

Richard thought about it for a minute and then said, "Yeah, I know where it is. I'll be up in a day or two." And then he turned and walked away, still cursing the man who had killed his dog.

I waited a week, and then another. Bug Sur is like that. You can never be in too much of a hurry because things get done sooner or later, or they don't. Nobody gets too concerned.

About three weeks later I saw Richard again at the post office. I figured in his anger of the dog-killing incident he had probably forgotten about me, so I went up and said hello. "Remember me? The washing machine on Partington?"

"Wanta go to Alaska with me and fish for salmon?" he asked.

"Well...sure...I'd like that, but I'm sort of married at the moment, and I really just need help with a washer."

"Yeah, oK," he said gloomily. "If I don't go to Alaska I'll be over in a day or two."

I doubted it, but to my surprise several mornings later there was a knock on the door and I opened it to find two men; one was Richard, looking as glum as ever, and the other was a tall, thin, dark-haired fellow named Hal Newell. I knew of his father, Gordon Newell, because we showed his marble sculptures at the Gallery.

"Laurel and Hardy Construction," Richard announced. "At your service."

I showed them the washing machine and explained that I didn't know how to attach the plumbing to it. Laurel and Hardy studied the situation for a few minutes and then went out into the yard and came back dragging our garden hose, still attached to the tap outside. Next they ran an extension cord into the front door of the house and plugged it in beside my bed. They then turned on the garden hose and started filling the washer up. "There you go," said Richard, looking quite pleased with himself.

I could only stand there staring. I guess I could have had the machine going weeks ago if I had only thought of this system, but somehow I'd had something a little more sophisticated in mind.

"Let me get this straight," I said. "First I go outside and drag in the hose. Then I get an extension cord and drag it into the living room. Then I turn on the hose. Then I turn on the machine, fill it up, and then run back outside and turn the hose off when it's full?"

"You'd better use cold water Cheer, and, of course, you'll have to repeat the process for the rinse cycle."

"Amazing." I said. "Do I owe you anything for this?"

"Do you have any beer?" the thin man asked.

"No, sorry, we're all out."

"Then just give us a couple of bucks," said Richard. "We're extremely hung over and we have to go down to the bar now."

XV
Out of the Frying Pan, Into the Fire

As time went on I was becoming more and more resentful of my situation. I would come home from work to be greeted by Robin, quite pleased with himself for having done some huge exotic abstract, and my stomach would cramp into a knot.

"The people don't want abstracts, Robin. They want seascapes. Small, affordable watercolors of the coast. Something to stick in a suitcase and take home for a souvenir."

"I'm sick of doing that rubbish," he'd scowl. "I cannae be bothered with pretty wee scenes. I'm trying to work on paintings for a one-man show."

"And I'm trying to work on paying the rent and feeding us. The car just barely works. I'm making clothes out of old bedspreads. I could use a little goddamn help!"

And so we'd snap at each other for awhile, and as the days went by, Robin lived more and more in his corner of the house and took to sleeping on the porch and going off to visit Kevin in the evening when he felt like talking to someone.

Finally one day I confronted him. "Would you be happier in Scotland...in a city...San Francisco, maybe?"

"No, I don't want to go back to Scotland, but I would like to be someplace where people appreciate good art."

"Canada maybe? Washington...Port Townsend, Vancouver? You have friends up north."

"Maybe."

"OK. I'll make you a deal. You go to Washington or Canada or wherever. Visit your friends. Look around...check the art world out. If you can sell your stuff up there or get some kind of a job and find us a place to live, Jamie and I will move there. I'll buy you a ticket with my next paycheck."

"What, you want me to go up there on my own?"

"I've got to work and pay the rent on this place. You're a big boy. You can handle it. Things have got to change in this relationship, so you better start thinking about it."

Robin was none too thrilled with this plan, as he was perfectly happy to go on forever living in his little bubble of oblivion at the other end of the house, but he knew that if he did not do something to appease me I'd either be packing him up and shipping him out, or shipping out myself, so he agreed to go. Two weeks later Jamie and I drove him into Monterey and loaded him onto a northbound Greyhound bus.

It was absolutely incredible the weight I felt had been lifted from my shoulders. I went to Longs Drug Store, and with the money I had left over from buying the bus ticket, I bought a bottle of tequila, a deck chair and a trashy romance novel.

Jamie chose some M&M's and a box of Leggo bricks, and we went off the the beach to celebrate. At least *I* was celebrating. Jamie was a little sad and puzzled over the sight of his dad boarding the bus, obviously not happy at being shipped off to parts unknown. I tried to make light of it, telling him we'd have lots of good times together, that his daddy was off on a big adventure and would be calling soon to tell us about it.

The party people didn't come around much after Robin was gone.

They had sense enough to know that trouble was brewing and they left me alone to my space, with the exception of Alan, who stopped by from time to time to show me some sort of treasure he had come across on his bicycle trips up and down the highway. My evenings were wonderfully peaceful and I began to relax and enjoy life as a single parent.

At work one day, Larry asked me if I was going to the Libra sign party at Nepenthe. "You're a Libra aren't you? You should go. Sign parties are fun. All the birthday people get free cake."

I had been to Nepenthe a number of times for special occasion lunches or dinners, but not having much money we did not frequent the bars so I was not really up on the Big Sur night life. I thought about it, and it did sound like it might be fun. "What about Jamie?" I said.

"Oh, everyone brings their kids. He'll love it," said Larry. And so that night my son and I ventured out shyly, to join the crowd at the Nepenthe bar.

Nepenthe was home for a lot of the Big Sur residents. Some of them lived around in the back of the building and ate at the family kitchen where Lolly Fascett, the owner, fed and mothered the homeless. Some of them just lived on bar stools all day and slept in their cars in the parking lot at night.

At the bar I spotted the Parson boys, already working hard on picking a fight. Larry and Louise and some other folks I knew were at the birthday table. Jamie saw a boy he knew from the Gazebo and went off to play on the terrace with him, so I sat down at the bar and ordered a glass of white wine. At the sound of my voice the man on the next bar stool turned toward me, and I saw it was Richard Trotter. "How's the washing machine?" he asked.

"It's OK. I thought you were going to Alaska."

"Na. I'm trying to decide whether or not to get back with my old lady and my kid."

"You have a wife?"

"I have a couple of 'em, and a couple of kids."

"Oh, I didn't know that."

"Where's your artist?"

"He's out of town for awhile."

Richard thought this information over for a moment. "Wanta fuck?" he said.

I was flabbergasted. Nobody had ever been quite so blunt with me before. "I...well...I just got here," I said at last, feeling that this was most certainly the wrong answer. Maybe I should slap him, but he seemed so nonchalant about it that I figured it must be a joke.

He shrugged his shoulders. "Maybe later," he said. "Watch my drink for me while I go for a pee."

The Trotters were definitely something else again, but after four years in Big Sur I was getting used to surprises. I waited quite awhile for Richard to return but he seemed to be taking his time in the bathroom. Finally I saw him across the room chatting with some people, so I left his drink to fend for itself and wandered out onto the patio to check on Jamie.

There was music playing and people dancing...some with each other, some alone. The moon was big and bright, sparkling over the ocean. I felt a weird combination of freedom and loneliness. This would be the perfect time, and the perfect place to be with the perfect man, dancing out on the veranda in the moonlight. But I had no man. My husband was hundreds of miles away and I didn't miss him. I felt like a tiny dark speck on the edge of the endless ocean that spread out for miles and miles in front of me.

Someone tapped me on the shoulder and I jumped. It was Larry. "Come on, Krissy, it's time for the cake. I'll introduce you to all the crazy Libra people."

"I'm afraid to go back in there," I said. "I told Richard Trotter I'd watch his drink and I didn't do it."

"Oh, don't worry," said Larry. "He'll probably just come over and flatten your house with a big Caterpillar tractor or something. Richard's nuts."

"He asked me if I want to...have sex with him," I said.

"EXCELLENT!" Larry cried. "Now you don't have to worry about the tractor. He likes you. Isn't this fun!"

A month went by and Robin began calling from time to time, asking if he could come home yet. Another month went by and the people he was staying with began calling to ask me the same question. They didn't seem to get it. He felt he had been exiled and I thought he was on a mission to save our marriage, or at least find himself a new stimulating environment that would offer him a productive and profitable alternative to Big Sur. Apparently he was just sitting around up in Canada hoping that one of these days I'd come to my senses and send him a bus ticket back home.

Meanwhile, in Monterey Peninsula Hospital, Richard Trotter's sister, Phyllis, was suffering through the last stages of cancer. After going in to visit her Richard took to coming by my house to brood about the unfairness of life and the problems he was having with his "old lady" and how much he just wanted to buy a fishing boat and sail away.

No two people on this planet were ever more different than Richard and I. In my youth, and even still today, it was hard to get through a sentence without having my mother correct my grammar. And in her opinion, persons who raised their voices or showed any signs of being aggressive or violent were considered lower-class, ill-mannered boors. Richard was all of these things and more. He was a Vietnam Vet, a barroom bullshitter and a womanizer. Worst of all, he had a tattoo of a drunk raccoon on his bicep.

I, on the other hand, had always sort of fancied myself as the Lady of Shallot, drifting down the river in long, flowing skirts, marching for peace, and rescuing homeless animals. One friend who saw us together at the local store said, "So what's the connection? Is he a closet intellectual or are you a closet bumpkin?" Another one just shook his head sadly and said to me, "So it's out of the frying pan into the fire, eh?"

I had no idea at all what was happening. All I knew was that my relationship with my husband had gone sour and I was sick of trying to fix it. If this was the wheels of karma in motion, then let them come ahead and run me down because I was too weak to object, and besides it was rather new and exciting to be courted by a beast.

Firewood was no longer a problem. Car troubles? Nothing a little bailing wire and some duct tape wouldn't fix. Hungry? We'll just row out into the crashing surf and murder a few dozen rock cod.

Pioneers have no fears...there's a solution to everything. I had never been taken care of. I was always too busy taking care of everyone else. It was a welcome change, and by the time Robin figured out how to get back home, I had decided I could not go back to living with him.

"I'll just sleep out on the porch then, will I?" he suggested hopefully.

"No, Robin."

"The wee tree house would do, maybe, and I could just pop in during the day while you're out and do some painting in the studio."

"No. You have to move." I felt so horrible and depressed trying to explain things to him, and he didn't make it easy.

The situation with Richard had him as baffled as it seemed to have everyone else. "Why a Neanderthal, Kristin?" he asked. "I could understand you wanting another man...but him...a barbarian, a cave man...the missing link...I never thought you were like this."

"Think about it, Robin." I sighed. "It's precisely because he *is* the missing link. The missing link between being the caregiver and the caregetter...between money and the lack of it. I'm sick of busting my ass trying to make ends meet while you sit around resenting the fact that nobody realizes you're a genius. Maybe I'm a goddamn genius, too, and I just never had the time to find out. I'm tired of resenting *you*. You've just got to try and make it on your own."

Shaken and perplexed, Robin once again allowed me to pack his bags, find him a temporary place to live, rent free, and move him into it.

My heart was breaking as we stood there in his new home; a rundown shack on the rocky ledge at Krinkles Corner. "Look," I said, pointing out the lopsided window at a beautiful view of purple kelp weeds floating in the little turquoise bay, "you can paint all day long and nobody will bother you."

Robin was silent for awhile, and then he said, "When I was a boy my mum took me to hear Billy Graham speak in Glasgow. I got so caught up in what he was saying…so emotional…and at the end he was shouting, 'If you believe in Jesus, rise up and go with me!' I jumped out of my seat and started to run down the aisle, but my mum grabbed me back and said, 'For goodness sake, son, don't be daft!' I wanted so much to run away and join him."

I thought this over for a moment while I stood there watching the kelp bobbing up and down on the waves. "Maybe you should have gone for it, Rob. It's funny, isn't it, how your whole life might have been changed if you had reacted differently to just one single minute of it."

Suddenly the meaning of my words hit me like a ton of bricks. I turned around and hurried out of the cabin, while I still had the nerve, and I didn't look back.

XVI
Santa Lucia Ranch

In 1980, Richard and I moved south about seven miles to the Santa Lucia Ranch where we had gotten a job as caretakers; he as ranch foreman, and me, as the housekeeper. The job description stated that they wanted "a couple" for the position, so we made it official and became one.

The main house was a big Japanese-style building consisting of three bedrooms, a kitchen, and a huge living room with shiny black tile floors and one wall of solid glass that looked out over a man-made lake on which lily pads and elegant black swans floated.

This was the weekend country house of Bill Hudson, who was a Monterey businessman. He was in his late seventies, divorced and suffering from heart problems, so he did not come down to the Big Sur house much anymore. He did, however, spend a lot of time worrying about whether or not it was being properly taken care of. He sent friends and relatives down on holidays to enjoy the place for him and report back as to how well it was looking.

Our house, which was the caretaker's unit, was a wonderful two-bedroom house on the edge of Dolan Creek Canyon, overlooking miles of coastline and sea. Its living room, kitchen, gas heating and hardwood floors were the closest thing to a *real* home that I had seen since my childhood, and best of all, we were being paid to live there.

Not only did we have a beautiful home, but the job provided us with two ranch vehicles, a pickup truck and a Jeep, a row boat for the lake, a private beach and 1,000 acres of land to live on. Things in my world were definitely looking up. Soon after we moved there, Richard's oldest son, Morgan, who was nine at the time, came to live with us and Jamie acquired a step-brother.

Town trips, too, were now very different, for we would take the pickup truck in to be loaded up with provisions for the ranch. As well as stocking up the main house, we would buy generous amounts of food and alcohol for ourselves, including a good bottle of gin and some tonic for the long ride home.

Life with Robin, whether we were on the best of terms or the worst, had generally been pretty quiet, but Richard's world was surrounded by a constant whirl of action. It took me a little time to get my bearings. For one thing, he had an insatiable appetite for sex. Most of Robin's sexual energy went into his art, and we had been on such ragged terms for so long that sex was rarely ever thought about, but to Richard it was not only part of the daily routine, it was a necessity, a ritual, the energizing drug, that like a shot in the arm, gave him the needed boost to jump out of bed and face the day.

At six in the morning all I wanted to do was roll over and go back to sleep for forty-five minutes before I had to get the kids up for school, but Richard was out and about, cursing and crashing and waging war on the morning with a vengeance.

"Goddamn fucking cats! Hey baby," he'd beat on the window, "you up yet? You should come out here and see what your goddamn cats did to my onions. They dug 'em all up and pissed all over the place. They think it's their goddamn litter box!"

Then he'd move along to the boy's side of the house. "Hey, kids!" Rap, rap, rap, on the window. "You need to get up and get out here and feed the goddamn pig before you go to school. One of the bantam chickens is missing, too. I tell you if that goddamn dog killed it, he's going over the cliff."

Back to our bedroom window again. "Hey, baby, you gonna put

that coffee on pretty soon? Did you hear me tell you about the garden? They got my carrot starts, too. I'm gonna kill those fuckers if they don't leave this garden alone."

And so I'd get up and start breakfast. Dogs and cats would greet me with anxious noses pressed against the glass door of the kitchen, wondering if all the threats made against them were true.

"Hey, throw a little brandy in that coffee, will you, baby!" Richard would shout. "Are the kids up yet? They'll miss the goddamn bus if they don't get their butts in gear."

One of the first major jobs on the agenda when we moved to the ranch was clearing the road to the beach, which had been taken out a few years back by a landslide. Soon after we moved in, Richard and I drove down the precarious little jeep trail to look at the damage, which turned out to be considerable.

A large section of the cliff face had broken off and slid across the little dirt road, covering the hillside all the way to the ocean below. It would take careful cat work to dig it out, and since it was such a steep slide of soft sandstone earth, the heavy equipment could roll and be buried in an instant if the slide chose to come down again as the soil was being moved.

Richard viewed the slide gloomily. He climbed around and checked it out from different angles. "Shit," he said. "This is going to be a motherfucker."

"Why don't you talk to your dad?" I suggested. His father, Frank, was as big as his younger brother, Walter, but a lot more gentle and cheerful. Everyone in the community loved him and referred to him as "Poppy," or "Uncle Frank." I figured since he not only had a lot of experience in this sort of thing, but was also Richard's father, he would be the obvious one to call.

"I don't talk to my dad," Richard replied. "He doesn't like me. I'll figure this thing out myself."

I could tell the slide had him worried. He busied himself with a lot of other jobs on the ranch. Every day or so he'd hike down and look at the beach road and come back depressed.

Bill Hudson was getting impatient. He called often to see what progress was being made. He had ultimate confidence in the pioneer families of Big Sur, fully trusting that if anyone could move mountains, they could.

Richard's mother, Fern, was cooking for the Ventana Deli at the time, making up big batches of her famous chili that included among other interesting ingredients, tequila and chocolate. As well as her chili, she was also famous locally for performing at local grange programs and talent shows where she would play "The South Coast Waltz," a favorite of old-time residents and homesteaders on her accordian.

One day when I stopped by the deli to pick up some French bread and cold cuts, I slipped back into the kitchen to chat with her.

"Hi, honey," she said, leaning over her bubbling cauldron. "How are you kids doing down at the ranch?"

"Richard's got a problem with a big slide down by the beach," I said. "I wish he'd call his dad to come out and take a look at it, but he won't. He's too proud to ask anyone for help. I'm afraid if he tackles it alone he'll be buried alive."

"Damn silly men," she said. "I'll talk to Frank about it. Just don't you worry, honey."

Sure enough, the next morning, bright and early, Frank's old gray pickup truck rolled into the driveway.

"Wonder what the hell he wants?" Richard mumbled. "You didn't call him did you, 'cause I'm really gonna be pissed off it you did."

"I didn't call him." It wasn't a lie. I'd only talked to his mother.

Frank had been hurt years before in a car accident and he still limped badly, dipping one side of his body up and down like a seesaw as he walked. I went out to greet him and he handed me a plastic bag full of hard candies. "Brought these for the kids," he said.

Richard appeared in the door behind me, but he didn't speak.

"So," said his dad. "You're the foreman now."

"Yup," said Richard.

"Guess they had a bad slide down here awhile back."

"Yup. I'm goin' out to work on it today."

"Let's take a look at it," said Frank.

Richard glared at me. "You did this," he whispered.

"I did NOT," I said.

The two men climbed into the Jeep and headed down the road. Half an hour later they were back, out in the yard, fumbling with the Caterpillar tractor and chatting about diesel fuel or something. Richard called in for coffee and I put the kettle on. Things seemed to be going well.

When I took the coffee out, I said, "Well, guys, what's the verdict?"

"Dad's gonna do it for me," said Richard. "He doesn't trust me."

"I trust you," his father said. "I just don't want you to screw it up."

"Which means, you don't trust me," said Richard.

The two of them started to laugh. Believe it or not, this was a big breakthrough. From that day on Frank always stopped by the ranch on his trips south, bringing treats for the kids and checking to see if Richard needed any help with projects.

"It's great that the two of you are getting along so well," I told Richard one day.

"Hell, it's not because he likes *me*, it's 'cause he likes you," he said.

XVII
Bed and Breakfast

As well as taking care of business at the ranch, Richard was a sort of ambassador of goodwill on the long stretch of Big Sur highway, always stopping to help stranded motorists, foreign hitchhikers, homeless wanderers or down-and-out locals. More likely than not they would eventually end up in our living room, staying for dinner, sleeping overnight, and in several cases lingering on for weeks and even months. His mother claimed that this was a family tradition and he came by it naturally.

I soon learned to have a pot of soup or stew cooking on the back burner at all times, as we were almost certain to be setting an extra plate at the table for either breakfast, lunch, dinner, or all of the above.

One of our first visitors was Paradise Ed, who had stopped in for a few minutes to say "Hi" to Richard and tell us about his recent trip to Mexico. Ed ended up sleeping on the living room sofa for four months.

Before taking up residence at the ranch he had been living on a beach in the small Mexican town of Barra. He never stopped raving about the beauty and simplicity of the lifestyle there. "Paradise!" he'd say. "You sleep on the beach, fish for your food, lots of pretty girls and beer...no pressures...no problems...just paradise!"

So why, I wondered, had he ever left? With paradise behind him now, he seemed to be a man without a country; no car, no job, no home, no motivation...so he just hung around the ranch, helping with chores, fishing off the beach, and rolling the old sleeping bag out on the sofa at night. To his credit I will say that he taught me how to make a really excellent seafood cioppino.

The only other thing I can remember about Ed is that he liked to tell a story about a dog his family had owned when he was a baby. The dog had saved his life by biting his diaper and dragging him away from the Salinas River when he was about to toddle in. I think Ed later moved to Fresno...a far cry from paradise.

Next came Fisherman John, a redbearded Irishman who skiff-fished rock cod off the coast near Santa Lucia. He was tired of driving down from Monterey every day to go fishing and wondered if the ranch had any place he could put his trailer. It did, and John came to live with us for the next two years.

He was a cheerful, hardworking fellow with a lot of radical political and religious beliefs. He always received a lot of strange, controversial material in the mail. Among other things, he believed that there was no such thing as evolution, that the human race had come to earth by flying saucer. This always made for some lively discussions at the dinner table...me being shacked up with the missing link and all.

In and amongst Paradise Ed and Fisherman John, there were hitchhikers from Italy, Germany, Russia and one boy from Burgundy, France, who waited out a three-day rain storm with us and gathered wild chanterelle mushrooms which he sauteed in wine and cream sauce every night for dinner.

There was Pottsey and P. B. Rivers, Brian and Brightsun and Crazy Peter, Brett, Heroin Butch, the Portuguese Limpet Pickers, and one of my personnel favorites, Lahcen, the man from Morocco.

I had just finished my chores down at the big house and had hiked back up the road to our place to get things started for dinner when I heard the dogs barking. I stuck my head out the door to see had "his own landscaping company" back East some place. In honor of Lahcen I am including this recipe.

Daurade Farcie

One 4-lb. cod, cleaned
1 lb. tomatoes, peeled and chopped
3 green peppers, sliced
2 onions, chopped fine
4 cloves garlic, chopped
1 Tbsp. coriander
2 Tbsps. fresh parsley
1 can pitted, sliced black olives
1/2 lemon rind, grated
1/2 tsp. ginger
1/2 tsp. saffron
1 cup water

Cook all except fish over low heat for twenty minutes. Put half of mixture inside fish and bake in a greased baking dish for 45 minutes. Heat other half of mixture and pour over baked fish before serving. I'd suggest serving it with rice or couscous, but of course, Lahcen preferred popovers.

XVIII
E.I.E.I.O.

Richard's generosity toward the homeless was not just limited to people. It was also extended to animals. We had come to the ranch with two cats and a dog, but not long after our arrival we acquired a blue-eyed malamute husky named Stewart, whose owners were moving to Europe, a black cat named Walter, who had come along with Richard's son, Morgan, when he moved in with us, eight chickens and a rooster, a pig named Wiggins that someone had given Richard, two horses belonging to the ladies down the highway who had no place to board them, and a Red Angus calf named Star, whose mother had rejected it at birth.

I had objected to the pig because I knew the day would come when Richard would decide the pig should become pork chops. I could not bear to get attached to the animal and then have to fry him up for dinner, so when Wiggins came to stay, Richard built his pen away from the ranch house where I wouldn't be able to see him, and I refused to take him the slops.

Richard had that all under control. He had friends in low places. The bus boys and dishwashers at the Nepenthe restaurant kept for us all the leftover garbage in a big bucket so Wiggins would have plenty to eat. Nepenthe's specialty was Ambrosia burgers or "Amby's" as we locals called them. They came with a special Amby sauce consisting of something like mayonnaise, mustard and catchup all mixed together. The house salad was a blue cheese concoction that Wiggins developed a special passion for.

After several months of Nepenthe slops being dumped into his trough, Wiggins refused to eat anything that did not have either Amby sauce or blue cheese dressing on it. He was a highly developed gourmet pig; all the more reason why I did not want to get to friendly with him.

I didn't even have a chance to object to Star. We had driven across the highway and up the hill to one of the ranches adjoining the Santa Lucia so Richard could talk to Ashton DePeyster, the owner, about some work that he needed done. I was sitting in the front seat of the truck when suddenly Richard opened the door and put a calf on my lap.

"What the hell is this?" I said. The little thing was struggling and licking me, his big eyes rolling around like crazy.

"He was just born this morning," Richard said. "The mom won't have anything to do with him. He'll die if we don't take care of him and Ashton doesn't want him."

"I can't do this, Richard. You'll just want to make steaks out of him someday."

"Nah. The kids can raise him and then sell him later on. Poor little guy."

"How does he get milk? Do I have to breast feed him or something?"

"You just get a big baby bottle for him. I'll show you how."

So Star came home with us. We made a little bed for him in the shed and the next day we went into town and stopped by the feed store for a giant baby bottle and some calf formula. The sales clerk told me that I would need to feed the animal every four hours, warm the formula and presumably even burp him afterwards.

Richard and the boys promised to help, but nobody seemed to be real eager to help out at two o'clock in the morning, so I'd stagger out to the shed in my bathrobe with a flashlight and a bottle of warm formula the size of a liter of wine and cuddle up with the calf. No wonder he thought I was his mama.

As time went on and his little legs grew stronger he would come out of the shed and cavort around in the yard with the dogs and children. He wasn't sure which one of these animals he was, but he certainly knew which one was his mommy, because when I'd call the kids in for dinner, dogs, cats, children and calf would all come charging into the living room. Star's hooves were not so steady on the hardwood floor. He came sliding in like a kid just learning to ice skate, his legs sliding under him every which way.

When he spotted me across the room, he'd skate his way gleefully over to me, leap into my lap, moo and roll his eyes lovingly. This went on until he was the size of a pickup truck, and although we tried to keep him out in a fenced-in field, he was a strong bugger. He'd break down the gate in order to come and butt his head against my bedroom window, trying to get in to me, which was kind of terrifying.

Things were not much better with Wiggins. As he got bigger and healthier, filled with leftover Amby burgers and salad with blue cheese dressing, he was getting feistier than ever and had developed a Houdini-like technique of escaping. From time to time hysterical neighbors would call us with reports that there was a wild pig running through their garden tearing up the geraniums.

Therefore, I was not too surprised when judgment day came for Wiggins. I made Richard promise that the children and I would not be involved. The 4H Club, we are NOT! If it had to be done, then he must do it when we were not around and clean it up, cut it up and put it in the freezer with no more said about it. He agreed.

I was making a French glace strawberry pie when he came in the kitchen door with the big carcass over his shoulder and flung it down on the big redwood dining room table. It was a beautiful, warm summer day, and I had been feeling so happy, rolling out pie crust, listening to Cat Stevens and singing, "Ride on the Peace Train," and now this!

He looked straight at me and at first I thought he might be going to cry, but he just said, "I'm sorry. I can't do this alone. You are going to have to help me."

It didn't look much like Wiggins anymore, thank God, and even if it had been recognizable, it was now dead and gone and I didn't want the poor fellow to have died in vain.

I got out my *Encyclopedia for Country Living* by Carla Emery (the best wedding present I ever got, by the way), and looked up pigs. Page 377, "How to cut up a pig." There was a perfect diagram of a thing that looked a lot like the body on my dining room table. It was all laid out for you in steps one, two, three, four, and five: fatback, chops, sausage, bacon and scrapple.

I propped the book up on a chair and we each grabbed a knife and went to work. I swear that animal made the best roast pork I have ever had, but, somehow, no matter how much seasoning you added to the sausage, or how much gravy you put on the chops, there was always a hint of blue cheese dressing and the children would look up sadly from their plates and say, "This is Wiggins, isn't it?"

XIX
Prisoners of Freedom

There are no real seasons to speak of in Big Sur because the weather is always rather mild, but when the winter rains come the road gets messy and the tourist traffic slows down a lot. Many times lightning storms hit the Los Padres forest, causing wild fires to sweep through the Santa Lucia Mountains, destroying hundreds of acres of timberland wilderness.

They used to say that Big Sur was seventy-five miles long and fifteen feet wide. At a rough count there are around thirty-five creeks that cross the highway between Carmel Highlands to the north and San Simeon to the south. With the sixty inches of rain we usually get between November and April, the creeks swell up and the hillsides start to slide, taking out bridges and huge sections of pavement and you're stuck until Cal Trans digs you out and rebuilds the road.

The second year we lived at the ranch there was a slide to the south at Villa Creek and to the north at Partington. Both slides were so big that they buried the road in tons of earth, closing down traffic in both directions for almost a year.

With the power lines down, all the refrigerators and freezers were defrosting. Stranded locals were pooling their supplies and having giant potluck dinners before the food went bad. Esalen Institute was just up the road from us. They had big bins full of rice, flour and other grains and a gas stove for baking bread. We had a winter garden which supplied us with some vegetables. Bill's big pantry was stocked with a lot of exotic gourmet stuff and plenty of wine and gin which we promised ourselves we would replace as soon as the road was open.

I had always made fun of Richard and his pioneer tendency to squirrel away canned goods for the winter, but now I could see how this was a natural survival instinct resulting from his having grown up in Big Sur. Never had I realized how many dishes one could create with canned corn. Corn chowder, corn fritters, corn pudding, succotash...I think I even tried to make corn cookies at one point.

During one of the storms, a smaller slide cut the kids off from Pacific Valley School for several weeks. I took on the role of home teacher for our boys and several other kids who lived up the road. The students told me they were studying slavery, prepositional phrases, fractions, and all sorts of other unpleasant things I didn't know much about, so I said, "Well, now you are going to learn about Celtic folklore, King Arthur, Merlin, Druids, Picts, standing stones, castles and the wee folk that live in the fairy hills in the Shetland Islands."

The children were wide-eyed. One little Mexican boy whose parents were caretakers for a home down by Burns Creek shook his head. He was not always sure of his English and he looked from one to the other of his classmates for an explanation, but they were as mystified as he was. They were game, however, and anything sounded better than slavery, so we launched into a Scottish book about a shipwrecked stranger who turned out to be one of the Selki folk, half man and half seal, who came ashore from time to time to lure a beautiful wife back to the kingdom below the sea.

I had a perfect attendance record, with my students sitting silent and fascinated around the living room as I read. At break time they went outside and rode bikes up and down the deserted highway, pretending to be motorcycles and sports cars, or they took turns in the row boat, sailing around on the little lake, terrorizing the black swans.

Finally P.G.& E. was able to restore our power, and helicopters started dropping in supplies. Later still, the steep narrow Nacimiento Road was cleared. It wound up through the mountains to the Hunter Ligget military base and Jolon, then down again to Paso Robles and 101. Town trips were again possible, but now it was a six-hour round-trip journey.

Restaurants, motels and gift shops were all closed and the owners worried that they would go bankrupt before the highway was repaired. The only people making any money were the Cal Trans crews and they were working triple time.

When one lane of highway one was finally opened to the public, Bill Hudson called to say he was coming down to the ranch to check out the damage. During our long, marooned months, we had tried, not too successfully, to ration Bill's pantry and liquor cupboard. Now with his pending arrival we had to make an emergency run into the Pacific Grove Discount Liquor Barn to try and replace what we had used.

To our horror we found that Bill had extremely expensive taste in wine. The Boards Gin (a case of the purple label, which was dry, and a case of the yellow label, which was sweet) was available, but some of the French Bordeaux and Pouilly Fuisse were not to be found anywhere, at any price. What with all the booze and tins of imported herring, hearts of palm, asparagus tips and Greek olives, our bank account was totally depleted.

XX
Oh, Holy Night

In spite of mudslides, uninvited guests and Richard's violent moods, life at the ranch was infinitely more comfortable than Partington Ridge had been. We bought a television that got one channel, sometimes, and a fake Persian rug from J.C. Penney's. Fisherman John cut an old steel tank in half and made us a hot tub, which like a giant cannibal soup pot, had to have a fire built under it in order to get hot, and an old wooden pallet frame inside to sit on so you wouldn't fry your ass, but to me, it was pure luxury.

At Christmas time I wanted to go down the road to Lucia where the monks at the Camaldolese Hermitage had a midnight mass service. I did not get the urge to go to church very often, but my life had changed so much that I really felt the need to rejoice and give thanks on Christmas Eve.

This proposal was greeted by boos from the boys and a shower of profanity from Richard, who hated Christianity and claimed to worship only Shiva, the god of destruction and reproduction. How appropriate. Still I persisted, reminding everyone that I had spoonfed them and every other person that happened to be in the house, catered to everyone's needs, washed and cleaned, not asking for a lot in return. Was it such a huge sacrifice to ask them for this one little thing? I finally won, and grudgingly they donned clean clothes and shuffled off to mass.

It was a long service, starting at eleven o'clock and going on for what seemed like hours. I tried to enjoy it but the children were restless and Richard kept slipping outside for a cigarette, so I decided that it had probably been a silly idea. When we finally got back to the ranch, the boys were trudging wearily off to bed and Richard happened to glance down the hill toward the big house.

"That's funny," he said. "There's a light on down there. Did you leave a light on today when you were cleaning?"

"I never turn the lights on in that house. With all those windows you don't need one."

"Hmmm. Bill wouldn't come down on Christmas and he would have told us if he was sending guests. Shit. I better hike down there and check."

He went in and grabbed the flashlight and went off down the hill, while I said goodnight to the boys and put on my robe. As an afterthought, I heated up the kettle for a brandy and lemon nightcap, because as grumpy as Richard was, I figured we'd need one. He was gone for quite awhile and I was starting to get worried when he finally came in and slammed the door.

"Church!" he said. "What a fucking great idea that was! God must be one hell of a groovy guy, you know. You oughta see that place. It's a goddam mess, the doors broken in, the cupboards all ransacked. There's broken bottles and shit all over the place."

I was horrified. We had never locked our doors the whole time we'd lived in Big Sur. There was the odd transient from time to time that might come in and help himself to a beer, but nobody was ever really robbed like this.

"Who would do something like that?" I said.

"Well, it sure as hell wasn't Santa Claus," said Richard, pouring himself a heavy shot of brandy. "I can't do much about it right now, but first thing in the morning I'm gonna take a rifle and go out and find the bastard and shoot him. Merry Christmas—Bang!"

It was amazing that our own house was untouched, with all the presents under the tree and plenty of food in the kitchen. Still, we had left the living room lights on and the two ranch vehicles in the yard, so perhaps they had thought someone was home here, while Bill's house was down there in the dark.

Next morning Richard was up before the sun. He walked over to Fisherman John's trailer to make sure he didn't go out to fish in case he was needed for a posse. John needed no convincing, but grabbed his own shotgun and off they went into the misty pink dawn of Christmas morning.

The boys were very excited when they woke up. It sort of detracted from the usual anticipation of present opening to think that we may be witnessing the murder of a burglar in our own back yard. I decided not to put on the tape of Christmas carols that I had set out to play. Somehow, "Joy to the World" did not seem too appropriate.

The vigilanties were gone for over an hour, and we were all pacing up and down in the front yard when we heard the shot. "Shit!" I screamed. "I can't believe it. He actually did it. He killed someone!"

"Or they've killed him," wailed Morgan. "I want to go find them. I want to see my dad."

"No. You guys just calm down. Everything's gonna be OK," I said shakily, not believing a word of it. "We have to stay close the the house. I guess I should call the police."

"Why didn't we do that in the first place, Mama?" asked Jamie.

"I don't know. Because they are clear off in Monterey, and folks out here just seem to take things into their own hands, I guess. I could call Pat though. I think I will."

Pat Chamberlain was one of the local highway patrolmen. He was married to Richard's cousin, which made him family. He and Richard had never really seen eye to eye, Richard being the black sheep, ne'er-do-well of the Trotter clan. I liked Pat, as did most of the other locals. They trusted him enough to call him to complain about hitchhikers invading their pot crop, or if the cocaine dealer was late for a delivery.

I apologized for disturbing him on Christmas morning and explained the situation.

"That crazy son-of-a-bitch," said Pat. "Why the hell didn't he call the sheriff?"

"You know how Richard is," I said.

At that moment the kids started yelling, "They're coming, they're coming."

They were indeed, and all three appeared to be alive and in one piece. John and Richard holding rifles ready, walked on either side of a small bedraggled looking tramp whose hands were tied behind his back. I reported this to Pat who promised to call the sheriff and hung up.

Richard took a seat on top of the thief and heaved a sigh of relief. Having been in a similar position many times myself, I knew there was not much chance of the burglar making a move to escape.

"Well, baby, we did it," he said grinning. "The dumb shit was camping about a half-mile away down on the edge of the cliff. How about a coffee and brandy?"

"Who fired the gun, Dad?" Morgan asked.

"That was John. The guy looked like he was gonna make a run for it when he saw us, so we gave him a little something to think twice about."

"There's all kinds of evidence down there, too," said John. "Bill's stuff is scattered all over his campsite. Looks like he drank about half a bottle of bourbon, too."

"I'll get the coffee," I said.

"You better call 9-1-1 while you're in there and get somebody to come and pick this guy up," Richard said. I told him I'd called Pat and that the sheriff was probably already on his way.

Richard nodded his approval and changed positions on the back of his prisoner. "Put a shot of brandy in that coffee, will you, baby, and you might as well bring one for this poor bastard, too. He'll need it."

Good old Richard. Next thing we know, he'll be inviting the guy to stay for dinner and overnight. I took the cups outside and Richard eased up a bit so the man could drink without choking to death. He thanked me sheepishly when I handed him the mug.

"I'm real sorry about this, ma'am," he said. "Real sorry."

"Why the hell didn't you just come up and knock on the door if you wanted something to eat or a couple of bucks? You could have walked right in here and taken something, without being such an asshole and tearing the place apart like that."

"I dunno. I never figured anybody'd give me anything. I never asked fer nuthin'. I just steal stuff when I need it. I wanted some money."

"Well, that's not the way we do things around here," Richard said. "Somebody does stuff like that they wind up dead. You're fuckin' lucky we didn't blow your balls off."

"I'm sorry. I'm really sorry," the man whimpered. "Don't kill me...please. They won't kill me, will they, ma'am?" He looked up at me miserably.

"I just serve the coffee around here," I said.

"Good," said Richard, "'cause we're ready for a refill."

After what seemed like hours, the sheriff arrived and the burglar was read his rights, handcuffed and placed in the back seat of the patrol car where he promptly threw up last night's bourbon and this morning's coffee and brandy all over the back seat.

"Jesus, what a Christmas," said the sheriff in disgust. "You got any paper towels?"

The little man was hauled away at last, and we went inside to have breakfast and unwrap presents. Needless to say, it was the last time I ever suggested midnight mass.

XXI
Motherlode

Not long after the burglar incident, Larry came by to visit us at the ranch. I had quit my job at the gallery some time ago to concentrate on my housekeeping duties. Larry, too, had left, moving to Monterey to work as a house painter by day, and a pot farmer by night.

As is so often the case, once you have lived any length of time in Big Sur, no place else is ever quite the same, so now he was back, wandering the coast, looking for a caretaking job or a goat shed to rent. He had finally left Louise, who was now pregnant with another man's child, and he had been hanging around Nepenthe in the evenings looking for a new prospect. It was great to see him again, catch up on all the old Coast Gallery gossip, and hear him roar with laughter at my tales of life at Santa Lucia.

"I can't believe you two ever ended up together," he chuckled. "You are such an unlikely couple."

"It's hard to explain," I said. "But at least he knows how to drive and he's a good provider."

"And look at where you guys get to live!" said Larry. "Shit, this place is beautiful!"

"Yeah, if you like running a homeless shelter. Richard brings home all walks of life to stay with us."

"Humm," said Larry.

"You want to live here?" I asked hopefully. "Hey, if Richard can invite people, so can I. It would be a welcome change...I'd have someone to talk to...philosophy, metaphysics, books, religion...it would be great...I could get my mind working again. What do you say?"

"Well, maybe just until I find some place permanent," he said. "I could kick in some money for food and sleep on the sofa for a week or two. I'm thinking of going down to Mill Creek to do some gold panning. Guys say they've found some pretty good sized flakes down there. Maybe I'll strike it rich."

And so Larry took up residence in our living room. The kids took to calling him Beulah because he did the dishes every day and helped tidy up around the house. Out on the front patio he set up his elaborate gold panning operation, consisting of buckets, sluices, hoses and screens. There he could be found every morning in his ratty old brown terrycloth bathrobe, with a cup of coffee, a cigarette, and a magnifying glass, searching for gold flakes in the daily bucket loads of sand that he hauled home from Mill Creek.

After four months on the sofa, Larry moved out back to a little rat-infested trailer that sat next to our tool shed. He ended up staying at the ranch nine months.

It was on one of the days when Larry and I were sitting around the sluice box discussing whether or not the Bible could have been accurately translated, since Jesus spoke Aramaic, which was a very complicated language with many different interpretational possibilities, that Keeker called me.

I had not spoken to her in some time, as she had been flown out by helicopter during the mud slides and had been afraid to return in case she got stranded again. She had gone back to the old cabin in Los Trancos Woods where we had first met to wait out the winter storms. Now she was back on Partington Ridge, and as usual, she had a problem.

"Oh, Krissy, my Keeker, I'm so depressed," she said. "I can't cope. I need you. Come and have a cup of tea with me."

DRINKING TO KINDNESS

As I think I mentioned earlier on, she had bought the house in the woods where my mother and I used to live so she could have some control over who her next-door neighbors would be. She had installed some friends of hers, a carpenter and his wife, and allowed them to live there rent free in exchange for various caretaking duties.

These "duties" had turned out to be a bit more than the young couple had bargained on, for they entailed such full scale projects as building a new deck, remodeling the kitchen and extending her house to include a sauna room. Finally tempers were starting to wear thin and everyone was on edge. Keeker was in a quandary because, after all, they *were* friends and one couldn't just throw them out, so after a great deal of agonizing, she had hit upon a solution which she wanted to discuss with me.

"You always loved that house, didn't you?" she asked me.

"It was my favorite! My first *real* home. I had my first boyfriend there, learned to drive, wrecked my mom's car, ran away, came back, read Kafka and Ginsberg and *Darma Bums*, listened to the Beatles and Dylan and Julian Bream, got busted, watched Kennedy's assassination, cut school a lot and tried to figure out what life was all about...and besides you were next door and you were so crazy and cool—what a role model."

"I was sooo fucked up, my dear, you cannot believe! But anyway, what I had decided to do was leave you that house in my will, but I'm not ready to die yet. In fact, I've decided to make my coffin into a planter box. But I just can't cope with caretaker bullshit, and so I've decided to give you the house now. I just can't deal with it...it can be *your* problem. Here's the deed. You'll probably have to go to a lawyer or a title company or some such nonsense and sign papers. Do whatever you have to do, but I don't want to think about it."

Just like that. Boom. Here's a house. Now take it and go away. Never in a million years had I thought I would ever own property. I had never had a job that paid more than seven dollars an hour. I drove an old rattletrap VW and had no bank accounts. My mother was in a similar state. Inheritance had never crossed my mind. Now, suddenly I owned a two-bedroom home in the hills behind Stanford

University...probably worth more money than I'd ever seen.

My first chore was to call the tenants and tell them that they now had a new landlady and I would need to ask them to start paying rent. They were astonished and furious, saying that if she wanted to get rid of the house so badly why hadn't she given it to them, who had done so much for her. I couldn't very well tell them that it was not the house, but the occupants that were the problem. They gave notice immediately, saying that they would be out by the end of the month, and I was left to find a renter for a house which was 200 miles away.

My second shock came not long afterwards when the property tax bill came. I had never even heard of property taxes and had no idea how I was going to come up with the $800 that was due in two months. I began to join Larry on the patio, scanning the gold pans and praying for a shiny flash to wash out of the sand.

In the middle of all this perplexing red tape that I was trying to unravel, something else happened at the ranch that was to change everything once again.

Bill Hudson came down on a Friday afternoon, bringing with him a young couple from San Francisco who we had met several times before. They loved getting away from the city to spend weekends with Bill at the ranch and he enjoyed chauffeuring them around the property in the little red Jeep and sitting by the lake in the evening sipping cocktails.

On Saturday morning the phone rang and it was Jan, Bill's guest, saying that Bill had not gotten up that morning. He was lying in bed with his eyes open, but he didn't seem to be able to move or speak. It appeared that he had suffered a stroke in the night. We called 911, and the last I saw of him he was being loaded into an ambulance on his way to Monterey hospital where he died.

Although we remained at the ranch for almost another year, it was the beginning of the end of the Santa Lucia Ranch days for us. Bill's son, who had been adventuring out on the high seas in his trimaran, came home and put the house up for sale. Richard and I began to look for someplace else to go.

XXII
The Church in the Wildwood

During the old mud slide days the Villa Creek road closure to the south had been cleared long before the Partington slide, and so town trips had been rerouted to San Luis Obispo County and the Cambria Paso Robles area instead of Monterey. The drive to Paso Robles to the closest supermarket took two hours, but driving down the coast past Piedros Blancos and San Simeon was beautiful and I liked the lazy feeling of that area better than the tourist atmosphere of Carmel and Monterey.

I remember when we'd take the last few bends in the highway, just past Ragged Point and get on the straighaway below Hearst Castle, I would feel myself start to relax and enjoy the surroundings.

I began to think how nice it would be to live a little closer to civilization, and for the kids to be able to go to a real school and get involved in some activities. I wondered how much property cost in the area. The house in Los Trancos Woods was too far away from our world which revolved around the Big Sur coast, and I had been considering selling it. For the short amount of time I had been a home owner and landlord, I had come to agree with Keeker that it was no fun at all.

Meanwhile, Richard had been busy chatting with his cousins, the

Harlan boys, who ran Lucia Lodge, several miles south of the ranch. It seemed that they were wanting to build a bar under the existing restaurant which would require a lot of excavation on a hillside too steep for heavy equipment. It was a job for a giant mole, or a Trotter with a wheelbarrow.

They offered to let us live in the only available staff housing on the property. It was a run-down trailer with a little room built on to the side of it where old Glen Harlan had once held his revival meetings. A weather-beaten wooden sign on the front proclaimed it to be "The Church in the Wildwood." At this point, the congregation seemed to consist of nothing but a bunch of pack rats. Their nests and droppings were in every conceivable cupboard and corner, including the oven, which reeked of mouse pee. Lucia was below the P.G.& E. power line cut off. The restaurant and lodge operated off of a generator, but the church had only an oil light and some candles.

Still, this was Big Sur and we felt lucky to have found both work and housing, so we plunged into the massive project of cleaning up the church and making it livable for awhile. After the luxurious comforts of the ranch it was quite a challenge.

The only remnants of any sort of Christian worship having gone on there was in the added-on room, where a faded satin wall hanging, embroidered with a crucifix in gold and silver threads, hung over a raised platform that may once have been a pulpit, but now held a double bed.

Richard objected immediately, saying there was no way he was going to have sex on a goddam alter, but I insisted that it stay, as it was the only thing in the building that had been untouched by the gnawing teeth of rats and I thought perhaps it was good luck that they respected this particular area.

It was on this pulpit, by the light of a bright full moon in July, which set the rose-colored tapestry above the bed glowing, that our daughter was conceived.

Ken Harlan gave me a job working in the lodge office which served as a reservation desk and mini market for travelers and guests of the inn. Everything was ten times the price it should have been, including the cabins which had a nice view of the ocean, but had not been upgraded much since they were built in 1940, and "rustic," as they were described in the brochure was a definite glorification. Windows didn't quite shut. Bindweed vines had crept in through cracks and wound around the rafters and into closets and showers.

In the days when Ruth and John Harland had run the lodge, the generator had been turned off at nine o'clock at night and guests had to make do with candles, which many people thought gave the place its romantic charm. But when their sons Ken and Keith took over the management, they had upgraded the kitchen by putting in modern appliances, such as a big walk-in refrigerator that required the generator to be operated all night.

This did not please the honeymoon couples at all. They had paid ninety to a hundred dollars to drive two hours into the wilderness to find a secluded cottage where they could make love by candlelight to the sound of the crashing waves. Mostly all you could hear was the sound of the thundering generator. I was constantly accosted by angry, sleep-deprived couples with migraine headaches who demanded I give them their money back.

Ken's policy was that all sales were final. I would try to explain that, being sympathetic but firm, while pausing to run out the back door and throw up over the back railing as my morning sickness progressed. The trick was to be sure and try not to hit Richard as he passed by down below with the wheelbarrow.

Like every other establishment in Big Sur, the staff of the Lucia Lodge was unique. The gas station was operated by a Buddhist fellow named John, who when he wasn't pumping gas, was either chanting or taking furious notes that he said were being telepathically communicated to him by his Zen master who lived somewhere in Tibet.

The cook was a fat, rather glum-looking Eskimo named Sam, and the waiter, who also doubled as a cabin cleaner maid in the daytime, was a black man named Persay.

As is the case with so many people on the Big Sur coast, Persay had just been passing through on his way from San Francisco to Los Angeles when something had stopped him. I believe in his case, his Cadillac had broken down. He had been there ever since.

During the day he wore all white, from his shoes to his cap. He cleaned rooms, vacuuming and changing sheets, carefully collecting the odd bits and pieces that the guests had left behind. He once showed me a whole carton full of sexy underwear, open crotch teddies and other paraphernalia that he had saved, should anyone call for them.

At night Persay would totally change character. He took his job as a waiter very seriously. Wearing a black tuxedo and shiny black shoes, he would bow graciously to customers and glide smoothly from table to table with a bottle of champagne or a pepper grinder, giving almost no sign of recognition, had he happened to see you earlier on in his room-cleaning mode.

One of the many great Persay stories was that one day when he was in his "white" uniform he had gone to a room to put fresh towels in the bathroom, not knowing that the room was already occupied. As he opened the door he was just in time to witness a naked man leaping off of the chest of drawers onto the body of his wife, who lay spread-eagled on the bed, ready to receive him.

"Well done!" Persy cried to the horrified couple. He then left the towels on the chair and exited quickly.

That night at dinner the couple was horried to find that the man who had caught them in their energetic love act was also to be their waiter. But Persay, true to form and dressed impeccably in the old black tuxedo, bowed and took their orders without showing the slightest hint of ever having seen them before. I believe he received quite a substantial tip for his tact.

Life at Lucia was never dull, and with the harvest season coming on, helicopters buzzed Gorda Mountain and the Los Padres Forest every day looking for pot patches. As my pregnancy progressed, I became more and more determined to find my family a permanent home in a healthier environment.

When I worked at the Coast Gallery, I had gotten to know a group of artists who owned 150 acres in partnership on the beautiful 25-

mile stretch of rolling hills between Cambria and Paso Robles known as Green Valley Road. Now one of the couples was having marital problems and had decided to sell out their fifty-acre interest in the partnership. Knowing I had been looking around at real estate in the area, they suggested I come down one weekend when they were doing a craft show in Santa Barbara. My family and I could camp out at their place and see whether or not we were at all interested in the area.

It took forever to find the driveway and the steep, narrow dirt road that they had roughly sketched on a scrap of paper with the map they'd sent me. We wound down into the canyon and once we got to the bottom, we found that the creek was so high that it was not possible to ford it. We had to wade across to the only building we could see, which turned out to be a barn where the couple and their two children lived.

After the months we'd spent living in the mouse-infested church, I had hoped for something a little less primitive. I figured that if I sold the house in Los Trancos Woods I could afford to buy a three-bedroom house in San Luis County with a couple of acres of garden and maybe even a hot tub. This barn thing was not what I'd had in mind, still, once our eyes adjusted to the dark inside, it seemed cozy enough with a braided rug, rocking chair and wood burning stove.

Upstairs the sleeping loft had a tin roof, a double bed mattress on the floor and two cots for the kids. There was no indoor plumbing, no electricity, no insulation, and no proper access road. It would take forever and cost plenty to make the necessary improvements. Besides, I didn't fancy the idea of getting tied up in a partnership with a bunch of crazy artists. The whole thing was absurd. Three months later, I owned it.

XXIII
Rocky Creek Barn

Richard could not quite grasp the idea that we no longer lived in Big Sur. He still made the two-hour drive up the twisty highway to work at Lucia Lodge or Pacific Valley, or went off to Mill Creek to go out at five in the morning with the dory fishermen. I could not convince him that surely somewhere in our new surroundings there must be construction work to be found. And, of course, he never came home alone. Always there was the odd hitchhiker or Big Sur wanderer who had come for dinner, bed and breakfast. Barefoot and pregnant, I served up the meals and hauled the menfolk's washing off to the local laundromat, stopping on the way home to fill their orders for cigarettes and beer.

On one of our hiking trips around the property, we had found a small cabin about the size of a large closet, hidden in the oak trees on the top of the hill. This had apparently been a refuge for one of the dissolutioned partners who had owned the property last. I did not want any of our transient guests to find out about it because I had hopes of making it a sort of meditation hermitage where I could escape during the day and be alone to think for awhile.

But now came the problem of trying to arrange for Jamie to have visiting days with his father. Robin had gone from the shack at

DRINKING TO KINDNESS

Krinkles Corner to living in a garage at Windover Estate, and he now seemed to be traveling around with someone known as Blue Truck Chuck, who lived on disability and camped out at various vista points along Highway One. It was hard to know which turnout they might be living at from one week to another, and if we did manage to find them, Robin was always either drunk or in the depths of depression and would launch into a long and tearful lecture on how I'd ruined his life, while Chuck and his scruffy young son stood on the sidelines staring stupidly. I could never bring myself to allowing Jamie to become a part of their team, even for a weekend.

Richard and I discussed this as Easter vacation drew near and Jamie began to ask if he was going to see his dad. What if Robin were to come and stay in the little cabin on the hill? He and Jamie could camp out together for a few days. Robin would be nowhere near a bar and my son would be safe here on the property, close to home.

Richard agreed and Robin was located. He and Jamie back packed up the mountain with enough firewood, candles and food to sustain the two of them for a week. The week dragged on into another…and another. School was back in session and I came home from the store one day to find Jamie loading food from our cupboard into a pack to take up the hill to Robin, who had not yet ever emerged from the woods.

"My dad likes it here," Jamie said happily. "He's getting inspired to paint again, and he's given me a list of watercolors that he wants you to buy for him."

If I had owned a gun and had not been eight-and-a-half months pregnant, I would have climbed up the mountain and shot him. How dare he! And where the hell was my husband when I needed him? Out recruiting more vagrants to bring home, no doubt. How on earth had I allowed myself to get into this mess—again!

In April my daughter, Carmen Mariah, was born, and from that day on things began to change for Richard and me. He was beside me during her caesarean birth, managed not to faint when her sticky little newborn body was handed over to him and proudly bathed her and put on her first diapers.

"Isn't she beautiful?" I said, when he finally handed her to me to be fed. "I hope I won't have to stay here long. I can't wait to take her home."

"I'm going up to Big Sur to deliver a septic tank this afternoon," Richard said. "I'll probably be gone for about a week, but I think Ron can come and pick you up."

"You're what?!" I said. "You mean you aren't going to stay home with the kids and come in and visit me?"

"Robin's there with the boys. They'll be OK," he said. "I've got the baby to think of now. I'm going to have to go up there and get some work happening to make some money."

I figured what he really wanted to do was get up to Nepenthe as fast as possible to tell everyone he had a new baby and be wined and dined by the boys at the bar. They'd welcome him home with open arms and he'd put all the deadbeats to work digging culverts and retaining walls and be back in his element again…the bighearted bullshitter that everyone relied on.

From then on Richard came home less and less and I spent weekdays with my two children, my stepson and my ex-husband, working on converting the barn into a real house. On weekends Richard would return with working partners in tow and he and Robin and the workers would nail a two-by-four here and there and sit around the oil lamp at night drinking beer and brandy and playing poker.

I wondered where he stayed and what he did on the weeknights he was away. He had a room, supposedly, in his parent's basement, but he was never there when I called. I felt lonely and depressed and used. I begged him to come home and find work closer to us, but he insisted that there was no money to be made in San Luis Obispo County and plenty of work in Big Sur.

Things began to get ugly. A friend called one day and informed me that when Richard worked up there he lived with a woman on Pfieffer Ridge. I confronted him with it and we tried to patch things up, but it was over. On Mother's Day we packed his bags together at

DRINKING TO KINDNESS

dawn and he left for Big Sur, permanently, before the children were awake. Like Frank and Walter and Sam, who had first homesteaded there, no place but Big Sur would ever be home for the Trotters.

XXIV
To Climb and Fall

To Climb and Fall and Climb Again

The westward sea and the warm west wind—
It was these, not I, that wrought my rhyme.
I, that have lived, and sorrowed, and sinned,
Have spoken no word of my life as it is;
Have spoken only the ocean's abyss,
Only the open waves, that kiss,
And climb on the cliff, and fall and climb.

Let them climb, and fall, and climb as they will;
It is one to me, who have made what I might
Of long loves gone wrong, and light loves gone ill,
And loves of men that witches have caught,
And loves enough, God wot; but not

The loves I have lived, nor the life I could write.

"Epilogue" by John Robinson Jeffers

DRINKING TO KINDNESS

I had thought I would be relieved to spend peaceful evenings alone with my children without the worry of wondering whether or not Richard was coming home, or in a bar, or hanging in his truck off of a cliff somewhere, but as time went on I grew more and more lonely and restless...hugging my pillow on moonlit nights and wishing I had another grownup to talk to.

Money was so low that we'd sit around after supper and roll pennies to try and accumulate enough for the next day's meal. The only phone calls I got were from my mother and bill collectors.

I got a job working part-time in a clothing store in the little art colony of Harmony, and I bought a book from the metaphysical bookstore on visualization, which promised to instruct me on how to make all the money I wanted, live the life I had always dreamed of, and to meet the perfect mate to enjoy it all with.

After dusting the shop and rearranging the racks of tie-dyed tee shirts and hand-woven shawls, I would sit down and faithfully do my visualization exercises. The trouble was I was never quite sure what I wanted. My son kept suggesting that I hobnob with the wealthy families who lived in Hidden Valley and had horse ranches and swimming pools and home computer systems, even Lear Jets, so he said, but I assured him they were not my type.

I began to meditate and try to focus on what I could do with my life. I seemed to recall that I had once had a very specific master plan, back in high school and college, but somehow it seemed to have dissolved in the Big Sur mists and floated off with the tide.

I began to doodle one day in the shop while practicing my visualization. I drew a picture of a dark-haired man with a beard, and then for some reason I gave him a funny little hat like a beret. I had him leaning up against the Harmony road sign and I then drew a rainbow over the town and and across the hills leading to my house. It was a silly picture, but I liked it, and I tacked it up on the wall behind the counter so I could study it and look for hidden meanings.

My friend, Mary, was working downstairs in the Wine Cellar

that day, and since the walls in the Old Creamery Building were just wooden slats, I could hear her swearing from time to time as she fought with the computerized cash register, which she seemed never to be able to master, no matter how hard she tried.

"Hey, Trotter, you up there?" she called to me.

"Yeah."

"What are you doing?"

"Visualizing perfection."

"Oh, shit! Forget it. Come down here; I gotta tell you about this little guy I met."

Mary was always going places and doing things and meeting men and then being disappointed by them. This would be nothing new, but I went down to chat anyway.

"So you met a cute little guy? How little was he?" I asked, leaning on the bar.

"Well, he wasn't *really* little. He was a trip. Really crazy. You'd like him."

"What makes you say that? I don't want to meet any crazy people. I'm sick of crazy people."

"OK, he's not crazy, but he's a wildman. I think he's Scottish or something. That's why I thought you'd like him. You used to live in Scotland, right?"

"This is getting worse by the minute," I said.

"His name is Alan, and he lives up in the hills in a tipi," she said. "I met him in the bar last night."

A person named Alan who lived up in the hills in a tipi? Surely it couldn't by MY Alan from Partington Ridge. Presumably he was still scampering up and down the cliffs of Easy Street in Big Sur. And he certainly wasn't a Scotsman.

"No, thanks," I said. "I don't want to meet any Scotsmen or any tipi-dwelling wildmen. I've been there and done that all before. Never again. Never!"

At that moment the man in my drawing came walking in the back door of the Creamery. He had black hair, a short beard, and he was wearing a dusty old tartan tam on his head. I looked at him in amazement, totally stunned, for he was most certainly the man in my rainbow picture.

He grinned, first at Mary, and then at me as he dusted off his clothes. "Sorry I'm so dirty," he said. "It's blowin' like hell up there on the mountain."

"Well, speak of the devil." Mary beamed at me. "We were just talking about you."

"Is this *him*?" I said in disbelief.

"I told you he was cute. I've gotta go wash glasses. You guys watch the counter for me. Say something in Scottish."

"Are you the one that used to live in Scotland?" he asked me.

"Yeah. I lived there for four years, but you don't sound Scottish."

"I'm Canadian. From Alberta, but my heart's in the highlands. I'm a Cameron…this is my clan tartan." He whipped off his tam and slapped it against his thigh, sending another cloud of dust into the air. "They were a fierce bunch, the Camerons. Fiercer than fierceness itself. IIIIEEEEE!" he cried, giving his rendition of a war cry. Several tourists turned around in alarm.

"But I'm very sensitive, too," he went on seriously, "and very spiritual. That's my Libra side, I guess."

"Oh, you're a Libra?" I said, getting interested in spite of myself. "I am, too. My birthday's September 28th."

"Mine's the 24th, so we're four days apart."

"Are you married?" I asked. I felt stupid, asking, but I couldn't help wondering if it was all just some weird coincidence or if Mary was trying to set me up with the guy.

"Separated. I guess we're getting a divorce."

"Me, too. Kids?"

"I have three."

"I have two."

We stood looking at each other for a minute, and then we started laughing. "So tell me about Scotland," he said. "I've never been there but I'd love to go someday."

"It's time for me to close the shop. You want a glass of wine?"

"I prefer Scotch. Why don't I meet you in the bar after you close?"

The first night we talked until three in the morning. It seemed there could never be enough hours in the day for all the things we had to say to each other. The second night he took me out to the Midstate Fair in his pickup truck loaded with four barking dogs in the back. He assured me that they would be fine sitting in the back while we toured the fairgounds and took in a concert.

We parked some place that would be easy to remember when the fair was over, but by midnight we were half drunk and tired and falling in love. We walked the streets of Paso Robles for two hours searching for the truck. Every now and then we'd whistle, hoping the dogs would respond and lead us to the spot, but unfortunately all the dogs in town from twenty different directions barked back at us, and when at last we located the vehicle, the dogs were sound asleep in the back and it was two o'clock in the morning.

Soon I was becoming a weekend squaw, spending cold, windy nights on the mountain top, huddled beside the tipi's smoking fire, wrapped in a Mexican blanket.

But in the end it was inevitable. The rainy season came on with a vengeance and the warrior and his tipi came down off the mountain to set up camp with me. Dogs, cats, children, and an ex-spouse gathered together by the shores of Rocky Creek, preparing to head boldly and blindly into what showed all the old warning signs of becoming another decade of madness.

The End

Author's Note

This book is taken from the journals I kept from 1974 to 1984: The Big Sur years. All of the characters are real and none of their names have been changed, so if I cause anyone to be angry or hurt any feelings it is unintentional. I love you all for having made my life so entertaining.

Alan and I still live here on the Central Coast Ranch that I fondly call Shanagolden in honor of Harrydick and Lillian Boss Ross. The children are grown and off on their own, and sadly, most of the people I've written about in these pages are gone now, but they live on in my daydreams, as I sit, beside Rocky Creek, watching the seasons change, sipping a glass of wine, and still drinking "to kindness."